Seeing with Music

Seeing with Music

The Lives of 3 *Blind African Musicians*

SIMON OTTENBERG

A Samuel & Althea Stroum Book

University of Washington Press   *Seattle & London*

*This book is published with the assistance of a grant from
the Stroum Book Fund, established through the generosity of
Samuel and Althea Stroum.*

Copyright © 1996 by the University of Washington Press
Printed in the United States of America
Designed by Audrey Meyer

LIBRARY OF CONGRESS CATALOGING-IN-PUBLICATION DATA
Ottenberg, Simon.
  Seeing with music : the lives of three blind African musicians / Simon
Ottenberg.
     p. cm.
  Includes bibliographical references (p.   ) and index.   Discography: p.
  Contents: Concepts—The setting—Sayo Kamara—Muctaru Mansaray—
Marehu Mansaray—The world of three kututeng musicians.
  ISBN 0-295-97525-3 (alk. paper)
  1. Blind musicians—Sierra Leone—Biography.   2. Kamara, Sayo.
3. Mansaray, Muctaru.   4. Mansaray, Marehu.   5. Mbira music—History
and criticism.   6. Music—Sierra Leone—History and criticism.   I. Title.
ML399.088   1996   786.8'5—dc20   95-49962   CIP

The paper used in this publication meets the minimum requirements of
American National Standard for Information Sciences—Permanence of
Paper for Printed Library Materials, ANSI Z39.48-1984.

In memory of Marehu Mansaray, Sayo Kamara,
and Muctaru Mansaray, three fine individuals and musicians

nthoro bena masala gbaleyum
Sorry, the Lord has appointed me a musician
—Kututeng song

Contents

Illustrations

Acknowledgments

I CARRIED OUT FIELD RESEARCH IN WARA WARA BAFODEA
chiefdom in northern Sierra Leone between October 1978 and July
1980 while living at the capital, Bafodea Town, in the southern part
of the chiefdom. The first year of my research was based on a fel-
lowship from the National Endowment for the Humanities, Washington, D.C., and the second part was carried out while I was on a
sabbatical leave from the University of Washington, Seattle. I wish
to thank both institutions for making the research possible, as well
as the Institute of African Studies, Fourah Bay College, University
of Sierra Leone, Freetown, which kindly appointed me a Research
Fellow.

In Bafodea Town, the three Kututeng musicians discussed
here—Sayo Kamara, Muctaru Mansaray, and Marehu Mansaray—
made my research not only a reality but also most enjoyable.
Without the help of Paul Hamidu Mansaray and Fatamata Mansaray, my two skilled field assistants, of Samba Kamara, my steward
and sometimes field aide, and of many other intelligent guides to
Limba culture, I could have accomplished nothing. I am also in-
debted to the late Paramount Chief Alimamy Mansaray of Wara
Wara Bafodea, who graciously accepted me as the only non-
African in the chiefdom at that time. The late Pa Salifu Mansaray,
one of the most respected elders in the chiefdom, whose compound area I lived in, was a source of great wisdom and gently
provided advice. I also wish to thank his son, Momodu Mansaray, now the Paramount Chief, for providing me with housing
and assistance in other helpful ways. Among others who particu-

larly contributed to the musical aspects of this study are Cootje van Oven, the doyen of Sierra Leone musical studies, Helen Stark, and professors Christopher DeCorse, Labelle Prussin, and Loretta Reinhardt, all of whom made helpful observations in the field.

In the United States, Larry Mericka and Gary Margason provided considerable technical assistance with regard to my Stellavox tape recorder and its use. Valerie Stains, an ethnomusicology graduate student at the University of Washington, assisted in some musical matters in a draft of this book. Salifu Kamara has made helpful comments on my spelling of the Limba language. Peter S. Davenport, another ethnomusicology student at the same university, wrote an excellent Master's thesis (1984) on the Kututeng music of Bafodea, based upon my tapes, field notes, and slides. Shortly afterward, he went to Bafodea to carry out his own musicological research, not limited to the music covered in this study but encompassing a wide variety of musical forms and instruments. I have drawn a great deal from his thesis to add technical musical comments to this book, and I am extremely grateful for his analysis, which much enhanced my understanding of Kututeng music and its performance. It had been my hope that we would publish our researches on the music jointly, but this has not been possible, and I do not draw from Davenport's field observations in this writing. Tapes of music from my 1978–80 research are in the archives of the Ethnomusicology Program, School of Music, University of Washington.

For the song texts reproduced in this book, I have employed a simplified phonetic transcription of the Bafodea Limba language, since my hearing is fading and my linguistic skills are minimal. Furthermore, there is no standardized written form of Limba, and very little has been written in that language. The basic Limba dictionary by Mary Clarke (1922) is in the Biriwa dialect, which is quite distinct from that found at Wara Wara Bafodea.

In late February and early March 1988, I returned with my wife to Bafodea for nine days while on a sabbatical leave from the University of Washington. We met two of the three musicians discussed here, Sayo Kamara and Marehu Mansaray, and heard them play Kututeng music, and I have incorporated data from that brief stay at Bafodea into this work. On that trip I had the help of Dr. Clarke Speed, then a graduate student in anthropology at the University of Washington, who was carrying out his own research on the neighboring Lokko (Landogo) peoples. I want to thank him and my wife, Carol, for their assistance. I also would like to thank professors Lois Ann Anderson and Christopher A. Waterman for reading the entire manuscript and for their extremely helpful comments on it.

As I finish writing in December 1994, a civil war has been going on in Sierra Leone for over three years. Fighting recently reached Kabala, only a short distance from my research site. Sierra Leone is crumbling as an organized state into political, economic, and human chaos. I hope this book will indicate that there is a very rich and warm human side to Sierra Leonean life, which I hope will come to the fore again.

Seeing with Music

1 Concepts

Music has been studied as a product of societies or of individuals,
but rarely as the product of individuals in society.
—John Blacking, *"The Value of Music in Human Experience"*

THIS WORK IS A STUDY OF THREE SIERRA LEONE MUSICIANS
and their musical performances among the Limba of Bafodea
Town and its environs in Wara Wara Bafodea chiefdom, northern
Sierra Leone. At the time of my research, all three men were blind,
mature in age, and known for playing the same instrument, the *kututeng*. Called elsewhere in Africa the *mbira* or *sanza* and by various
other terms, the kututeng is classed as a lamellaphone by ethnomusicologists (Berliner 1978:9, note *b*; Kauffman et al. 1980:402;
Kubik 1964; H. Tracey 1961) and is often mislabeled the thumb
piano or African piano.[1] Kauffman (1980:401) defines the lamellaphone as "a musical instrument whose sound is produced essentially by the vibration of thin lamellae (Lat. *lamella,* from *lamino:* a
thin plate or layer) or tongues of metal, wood, or other material."
A plucked idiophone, it belongs to a larger group of idiophone instruments. Because the same word is sometimes used for both an
instrument and its music at Wara Wara Bafodea, I write the term

1. General sources on this type of instrument in Africa are Beby (1975:80–
84), Borel (1986), Kauffman et al. (1980), Kubik (1964), and Nketia (1974:77–81).
Ankermann (1901:32–36, 89–91, map 3), Montandon (1919:26–44), and von
Hornbostel (1933:297) all provide early descriptions and classifications of the
instrument in Africa.

3

for the music with a capital first letter (e.g., Kututeng) and the name of the instrument itself in lowercase (kututeng).

I approach the topic of this music and its musicianship from the viewpoint of three performers' life experiences (Wachsmann 1970:132) and their problems in coping with the world as sightless, wifeless, and childless men who are poor and largely dependent on relatives for survival. Through their lives and work, I describe their relationships to their music, first for each musician in turn and then for the three together. In this way I reach a view of the men's music and its roles in their lives and in Wara Wara Bafodea society.

My approach is the reverse of what the ethnomusicologist Paul Berliner (1978) has done in his magnificent study of mbira music among the Shona of Zimbabwe, the most detailed analysis of this type of instrument and its music that we possess. Berliner focuses on the instrument and its music; only in his final chapter does he provide short (although intelligent and useful) biographical sketches of a number of mbira players, briefly relating the personal materials to the music itself. In contrast, I present three longer accounts of individual musicians, using these data as a core around which to place and understand their music. Berliner's more musicological approach, rather than an anthropological one like mine, is also employed by Cootje van Oven (1970, 1973–74, 1981, 1982) and by Judith Lamm (1968), the major writers on the music of Sierra Leone. Sievers (1992) provides a more technical introduction to Sierra Leone music.

I employ a view alternative to the well-established approach taken by Berliner and some other ethnomusicologists because I am an anthropologist unskilled in the technical aspects of musical analysis. I have, instead, a lifetime of experience in sociocultural anthropology, which moves me more toward the social aspects of music behavior. Ruth Stone (1982) argues for an integration of these two views—the sound-ethnomusicologist's approach and the behavior-ethnomusicologist's orientation—around the concept of music event (which I call performance). This integration would resolve problems of narrowness of interpretation. According to Stone (1982:16), "the sound-ethnomusicologist works at the micro-level, the behavior-ethnomusicologist at the macro-level." She goes on to write: "For the behavior-ethnomusicologist, music behavior results from the concepts or ideas that people have about what constitutes appropriate musical activity" (1982:18–19). I would classify myself essentially as a behavior-ethnomusicologist in Stone's scheme.

There is much to be said for a style of analysis which is grounded in exploring the past experiences of musical persons in a culture and which then looks at their musical performances through that frame, rather than starting with the instrument and its music. Because my approach stems from my being an anthropologist rather than an ethnomusicologist, I come to the technically more interesting aspects of the music only with the help of the researches of Peter S. Davenport (1984). There is also a tradition of scholarship on the behavior side of Stone's distinction, as in the work of David Ames (1973a, 1973b) and Christopher Waterman (1990) in Africa and in some of Alan Merriam's scholarship (1964, 1973, 1979).

My views also grow out of some of my previous anthropological writings. I am increasingly aware that some of what I have written in the past on African culture (Ottenberg 1968, 1971), although strong on the social structural and the cultural side, has allowed me too little room for exploring the experiences of the individual and has been too bound up with Western cultural values and hegemony concerning Third and Fourth World peoples (Clifford and Marcus 1986; Fabian 1983).[2] In both my more cultural and my more social anthropological approaches to research and writing, I have sometimes paid too little attention to the richness and diversity of individual experience. In this book, then, I focus on the lives and performances of three musicians with common knowledge of Kututeng. If my study differs at all from some others, it does so in

2. But see some of my more recent writings (Ottenberg 1988a, 1989a, 1989b, 1989c).

bringing to the surface the kinds of knowledge of individuals that research scholars often acquire in their fieldwork but suppress or bury in their analysis.

The musical aspects under study here are placed in the context of broader features: other types of music in the chiefdom, factors affecting the status of musicians and of blind persons in the society, rituals and performances involving music, and family, marriage, and work as viewed through the lives of these three men. Rather than abstracting the cultural aspects and minimizing the personal elements, I emphasize the personal as the element linking musical with cultural and social features.

Personhood and Agency

I wrote the first two drafts of this book in the early 1980s without making use of approaches then developing in anthropology around the concepts of *personhood* and *agency*, which have since crystallized. I find that my approach parallels the personhood-agency approach in some ways, and although I do not regularly employ these terms, my thinking for the final draft has been sharpened by the two concepts.

Personhood, or *person*, as some prefer to call it, arises out of anthropology's increasing focus on action and experience, where formerly it stressed social structure and cultural pattern. The emphasis is now on individual experience within culture, joining an actor-oriented approach to cultural structure. That is, a culture's rules of behavior and its religious, mythical, and other beliefs, which are a frame or cultural structure for the society, are not simply followed by members of the culture, as some earlier anthropologists viewed the matter. These rules are one aspect of personhood, particularly the rules about social roles, but people's behavior also involves various interpretations of the rules, of social roles, and of beliefs and myths, expressed in both thought and action according to individuals' needs and the situations in which they find themselves. People may violate, manipulate, and reinterpret these cultural elements and cause them to change (Jackson and Karp

1990). Members of cultures hold concepts of persons (Fortes 1973; Riesman 1986)—what persons are and how they should behave and conceive of themselves—that may be either general or specific to particular circumstances. Individuals may or may not follow the cultural rules to reach their goals, and whether they attain their goals or not, they act in their own self-interest.

The related concept, agency, developed by the British sociologist Anthony Giddens (1979), refers to this individual activity—the power of persons to accomplish things, to influence others, and to create changes in roles and rules. Agency has been employed to refer either to an influential person with power (Karp 1986:131n1) or to the everyday activities of ordinary people, as I will use the term. Using the agency-personhood approach also enables one to pay attention to the emotional states and feelings of individuals, which are important aspects of their agencies as they go about their lives. Yet the approach as it is employed in anthropology is largely nonpsychological (but see Riesman 1977, 1986).

The concepts of agency and personhood, which grow out of earlier, more formal models of culture held largely by American anthropologists and out of models of society held largely by British scholars, thus focus on the role of individuals in restating and re-creating culture and society as they go about the business of trying to satisfy their personal needs. Individual social actors play a more prominent role in the analysis than they did in the older anthropology. Anthropologists carrying out field research are themselves social actors with emotional states and behaviors, an agency that is part of the culture and society they study. Their actions and re-actions, which are now recognized not to be as objective as scholars once thought but, rather, frequently subjective, become part of the research. Insofar as anthropologists study Third and Fourth World peoples, they are often wealthier, have greater resources, and are likely to be influential persons with some local power. All of this understanding now needs to be integrated into the writing up of the anthropologist's research.

Ivan Karp (1986:131), reviewing the work of Giddens (1976, 1979, 1981) and drawing from the writings of Bourdieu (1977) and

Sahlins (1976), states that a goal for scholars should be "to examine how, in specific settings or social formations, structure is an emergent property of action at the same time that action presupposes structure as a necessary condition for its production." His emphasis is more on action, on agency, than previously had been the case in anthropology. Referring favorably to Giddens's work, Karp (1986:134) argues that Giddens believes that "the failure to consider action in the context of structure and structure in the context of action impoverishes both." My impression of the general trend of contemporary anthropological studies is that they stress individual action — that is, agency — more than structure at this time. There is an antistructural air about our profession at the moment, coming out of disappointments with the consequences of certain North American trends and with the anthropology that grew out of Durkheimian thought in Europe. In this book I have tried to strike a balance between structure and individual action, although I tend to fall more on the individual side in my analysis.

Further, Karp (1986:134) states that "Giddens takes the essentially Weberian position that action is intentional and goal directed." Thus, people's intentions are much involved in the idea of agency. This does not mean that individuals should be seen as having considerable freedom of action; that depends upon their social situation. They act and make choices in terms of the freedom permitted by the structure in which they live and the degree to which they can manipulate and move that structure to reorder it. And I believe that persons are sometimes compelled by their earlier training and experience to act in ways that may limit their ability to make choices even when the possibility of choices exists, and that at other times they are compelled to act against the rules. In any case, I do not believe that the directions in which individuals choose to move are based purely on materialistic motives, but that ideological and other factors also enter in (Sahlins 1976).

It should be clear that I do not consider structure to be rigid; it is itself a process, continually changing as a consequence of action. Quoting Giddens, Karp (1986:136) writes that "structure is both the medium and the outcome of action." Structure, according to

Karp (1986:136), "is always in the process of coming into being and never fully formed." I believe, however, that although the agency-oriented anthropologist or sociologist may regard structure in this social-science manner, it is a point to be discovered whether any or many of the people in a society being studied regard it this way themselves, rather than viewing structure as relatively rigid and unchanging.

These issues merge with current thinking about how to study performance in Africa and elsewhere. Margaret Thompson Drewal (1991:3), in her thorough review of African performance studies, writes of "three simultaneous paradigmatic shifts: (1) from structure to process (from an essentially spatialized, distanced, objectivist view to a temporal, participatory, interactive research practice); (2) from the normative to the particular and the historically situated (from the time-less to the time-centered); (3) from the collective to the agency of named individuals in the continuous flow of social interactions." The researcher is no longer a positivist studying people's behavior from a distant, uninvolved, "scientific" viewpoint (if he or she ever was). It is particular history and time that are significant, not the "ethnographic present" or the "ethnographic base line." The approach focuses more on the flow of individual behavior in performance than on collective action; the latter is the product of individual behaviors.

Drewal employs sophisticated terminology and concepts in her review, drawing from a wide variety of scholarly fields. Out of personal preference, I use a more pragmatic and particularistic approach to Kututeng performance, within a similar basic orientation. To me, Kututeng performance involves the musicians and their music, the responding chorus and dancers, the listeners, the sponsor of the performance, if any, and the interactions of all of these, as well as the time and setting of the performance, the relationships of particular Kututeng performances to others, and the relationships of Kututeng musicians to each other and to players of other instruments. It also involves the links of Kututeng music to other musical genres, rituals, and performances at Bafodea and elsewhere in Sierra Leone, to the general aesthetic of the arts at

Bafodea, to Bafodea culture at large, and to matters of social status. This represents a broad approach to performance (Stone 1982:22).

This approach leads to conceptions of differences and variations. Members of a culture interpret differently what the structure is composed of and how it should be regarded and behaved toward — even if the anthropologist tries to frame it as a coherent model. Even in quite highly structured and ruled societies, such as that of the Afikpo Igbo of Nigeria (formerly spelled Ibo), which I studied in the 1950s and in 1960 (Ottenberg 1968:240–44), there is considerable variation in individual action and in the interpretation of the model according to a person's social position and experience; the models that anthropologists create have sometimes been overstructured. The reasons individual and group interpretations of culture vary are complex (Merrill 1988:11–15) and involve individual life experiences, past relationships with parents, differing descent ties, varying economic and political factors, status differences, gender and age, individual skills, the nature of the changes going on, and so forth. The challenge is to explore and explain these reasons and not simply to ignore variations for the sake of the model or to see variations as exceptions to it, rather than incorporating them within it. The extent of these variations makes for a fascinating anthropology of interpretation but also for an extremely difficult one in analysis and presentation, because it pokes great holes in any model and makes difficult a systematic approach to the topic at hand.

Employing this view, I show the considerable diversity that exists within one aspect of Bafodea culture, Kututeng music. This diversity is a consequence of individual life histories, social change, the music's secular nature, and the fact that the learning of this music is not an inherited tradition, so there is no standardized tradition for teaching it. It also relates to psychological and biological experiences. The study of diversity in particular cultural aspects of society has been underemphasized in past anthropological writings in favor of a scholarly need to describe unities, to organize data systematically and rationally, and to systematize anthropological thought. What exists is a variety of individual experiences surrounding any cultural aspect such as Kututeng music. A body of music can be interpreted in a variety of ways by different musicians as well as by listeners. I am interested in doing so through an understanding of the lives of the Kututeng players. It is true that Kututeng, not being tied to religious rituals, may exhibit greater diversity than some other musical forms at Wara Wara Bafodea, yet, as we shall see, its performance is restricted by a variety of factors and there are limits to its diversity.

For the three musicians I studied, then, individual variation in musical and personal behavior is expected and occurs. In terms of cultural structure, there is Kututeng music itself: what is considered to be included in and excluded from the genre, the nature of its instrument, its aesthetics, what musical forms are expected to be played, what kinds of aesthetic criticisms of it are accepted and typical, and its place in the larger musical picture. In the realm of social structure, there are the expected relationships between Kututeng musicians in and out of performance, along with the general statuses and roles of both musicians and the blind in the chiefdom — what is expected of them and how they are to be treated.

In terms of personhood and agency, I look at how these three musicians cope with cultural and social structures and their rules, sometimes to adhere to them, sometimes to violate them, and at times to transform them. How do they rearrange the cultural model of Kututeng music and its social behavior? Do they alter culture and society by their actions? They may not so much attempt to alter society deliberately and consciously as simply to try improving their own lives. And does their playing as blind musicians in a society where most musicians are not blind change society's general conceptions of musicians and musicianship?

Kututeng is presented here not as a thing in itself but as a major aspect of the lives of three individual musicians playing the same type of instrument. This approach seems close to the way in which individuals actually live their music. It also permits me to view these three performers as part of the musical history of the area in which they live and to evaluate their particular roles in musical change. Whatever the situation may have been in past centuries, the present era is one of musical contact and innovation in Africa, even in the isolated chiefdom where I carried out my research. In my study of these musicians, I have had to consider this historical context because the character of the music is not static but constantly altering, shifting, and moving (Blacking 1971b). This work is also part of my larger analysis of the aesthetics of Limba rituals and various performances (Ottenberg 1988a, 1989b, 1993, 1994a); it draws on only a part of my research.

My general approach is fruitful for the analysis of many aspects of a culture. It seems particularly useful in studying individual creativity, including not only that of carvers, musicians, weavers, and other artists and performers but also that of political and religious leaders, adjudicators, and diviners—all cases in which personal skill is emphasized, creative choices must be made, and personal expression is involved.

The Impact of My Presence

An important part of this study concerns what I—a Western-born and educated, middle-class researcher with my own musical and scholarly experiences and with considerable wealth compared to most people with whom I interacted in the chiefdom—brought to the study of these three musicians and their music. What positive and negative features were created by my presence? What sorts of interactions did we have and in what way did I become an agent for cultural stimulation and change by interviewing musicians and others, arranging for musical performances at my home, some of which were taped, paying the performers, and hearing them play on other occasions? What influence on my research did these and related factors create? What emotional ties did I bring to my relationships with the musicians, and how did I affect their status, if at all?

In writing this account, I have included something of my own reactions to and interactions with the individuals concerned—the kinds of reactions that are often the basis of scholars' understanding of how they cope with the cultures they study. My own cultural distinctiveness, personal experiences, and personality become part of my way of understanding others' lives. My values, standards, and knowledge become the mechanisms for my perception of those lives. Insofar as I focus on individuals in this study, I must perforce give some play to myself as an individual; I cannot adequately do one without the other. Rather than trying to make my work "scientific" and "objective" by minimizing my cultural and personal differences from those whom I study, I have tried instead to bring these differences out consciously—to use them to better understand what is going on. I am not, however, writing an account like Chernoff's (1979) study of Ghanaian drumming, which includes much about his learning to play the music and about his relationships with his teachers: I did not learn to play the kututeng or any other instrument at Bafodea. The focus here is on three musicians, their lives, and their music, interlaced with some comments on my reactions to them and my role in their existence. I blend subjectivity with objectivity (Stone 1982:227–28), interpretation with objective observation. In my fieldwork as well as in my writing, there have inevitably been major swings back and forth between these poles. Surely this is where the skill of the anthropologist must lie: in showing an ability to dance intelligently between these differing perspectives.

It would be wrong to consider myself as having been passive in my relationships with these three musicians. We were all mature men of a certain age. I observed and asked questions, on occasion hired them to play, listened with care to their music and occasionally danced to it, enjoyed their company, drank palm wine with them, sometimes tape-recorded them, and in other ways interacted with them. Some of these behaviors are those that anyone who hired them might have followed, although the musicians were seldom hired. Others are aspects of my research. There are a few advantages to being a naïve observer and questioner, just as there are to being a thoroughly knowledgeable one. A gain for naïveté may be that, because I lacked training in a certain field, I sometimes asked questions that a specialist might take for granted. Moreover, I had considerable experience in anthropological field research before undertaking this project (Ottenberg 1990, 1994b). On the other hand, my lack of ethnomusicological knowledge led to some failures in querying and observing, as I discovered in discussing my research with Peter Davenport and other knowledgeable ethnomusicologists upon my return from the field.

I enjoy listening to Western classical music, particularly chamber music, and to traditional African music—not to speak of now-ancient Beatles melodies and some other musical forms. Yet Kututeng music, along with that of the xylophone and the *kora*, appeals to me more than many other kinds of African music because of its harmonic foundation, melodic qualities, and tuning system (Berliner 1978:41-42), which to my ear resemble those of some Western music.

At the insistence of my parents, I took piano lessons as a child at a rather pretentious music school, but they did not take. I also went to a social dancing school to learn steps and etiquette, and I enjoyed the music of big bands. My parents took me to chamber music concerts, and chamber music has remained a love of mine, as has opera. While carrying out research in Nigeria, I enjoyed Highlife music but have found the more recent Juju music and other newer forms to interest me less. Although I carried out some thirty months of research among the Igbo of Afikpo in Nigeria, starting as early as 1952, I never heard anyone play the Igbo form of kututeng, generally called the *ubo* or *ubo-aka*. It usually involves a gourd resonator with metal or wood tongues, the latter often bamboo strips.[3] I believe the ubo was only an occasional solo instrument in the Igbo areas where I traveled and in other parts of eastern Nigeria (Omibiyi 1977:19). I heard and enjoyed plenty of music in Igbo country, however, produced by various kinds of drums, wood and metal instruments, and raffia rattles, generally at rituals. But my tape recorder invariably failed, and my interests lay more in the visual arts at that time. Clearly, my limited Nigerian musical experience was of little assistance in Sierra Leone, other

3. See Berliner (1978:fig. 11); Borel (1986:152-53, fig. 100 [which is mislabeled as being from Kano, Nigeria]); Echezona (1980:20); Okosa (1962:5-6); Omibiyi (1977:19, 21 fig. 15); Thieme (1967:45-46, fig. 4).

than providing me with a sense of the importance of music as a component of African ritual and offering me enjoyment in dancing to it in my own clumsy fashion, to the delight and amusement of some people.

In the United States, I am more at ease with music strong in development and not overly repetitious—music lacking very complex rhythms and rhythmic alterations. I prefer relatively quiet music situations and behavior rather than loud performances with activity that approaches the violent, as in some rock music events and the like, and my taste has been for musical and dance performances only some two hours in length. All of these preferences are products of my life experiences and senior age. They frequently contrast with my African musical experience, where the music may be loud, with active behavior on the part of some audience members, and with activities lasting many hours. This contrast has forced me to develop dialogues with myself about musical aesthetic judgments. I have come to enjoy African music greatly when I am in Africa and music with different aesthetic qualities when in the United States. The setting of the music seems to be the crucial determinant for me. This dual orientation undoubtedly has informed my Kututeng research.

I am technically unskilled in music. In the field I had to restrict myself to making commonsense observations, to asking obvious questions, to thinking of my own Western musical experiences in relation to what I saw, heard, and taped. My background limited both intelligent communication with the musicians and the degree of musical comradeship open to me, as well as limiting my other interactions with them—in contrast to, say, Chernoff's (1979) or Berliner's (1978) situation. In writing up my materials, I have endeavored to make up some of these deficiencies through the assistance of Valerie Stains, who has had considerable experience in studying the mbira form of the instrument found in southern Africa, and of Peter Davenport (1984). Despite this helpful assistance, I alone am responsible for the outline and orientation of the work.

My understanding of the three men and their musical behavior not only was gained through the framework of cultural and personal differences between us but also was based on an attraction of similarities. I shared key qualities with the three musicians whom I studied: middle age, wifelessness—my spouse having died not too long before the research began—no regular female attachment, and childlessness. Like them, I carried out no food production and had no farms. In the field situation, although I was surrounded by many people, I was lonely for my own culture and people and for my late wife; the musicians' loneliness involved wishes for greater sociability and activity within their own world. And sometimes I was simply bored, as they were. I was not physically blind like them, but I was blind in a cultural and linguistic sense throughout at least part of my fieldwork, a stranger to their country. I, too, had problems in everyday coping, albeit not necessarily of the same kind and certainly not as serious as theirs. Although major distinctions separated us—my wealth and financial security, Western education, experience in the world at large, American culture, different kinds and levels of musical knowledge—it was the similarities, I believe, that attracted me to them and their life-style and led me to be sympathetic to their problems of coping.

The musicians' status in their culture was ambiguous, as we shall see. So was mine as a white stranger, the only one living in the chiefdom at the time and apparently the only Westerner ever to have much contact with the people of Bafodea chiefdom who was not out to do something to or for them—to change their lives, restructure their society, tell them what they should and should not do and believe in, or inform them of what was right and wrong. I was, further, the only "European" they had seen on a regular basis who was not religious and did not go to church, except for research ends. So I was an anomaly even among "Europeans" they had known. Thus, in different but perhaps parallel ways, the three musicians and I were oblique to the society. I believe it was these similarities among us that made our relationships go on so well and made field research with them so interesting for me and, I think, for them, too.

Yet there was a clear hegemony on my part in relationship to the three men. I could hire them to play for money and offer them drink in their loneliness, their freedom from other commitments, and their poverty. Through my patronage of them and my interest in their music, they could hope to gain improved status in the eyes of other Africans and perhaps in mine. These factors probably made it difficult for them to refuse my requests for music or talk. Certainly they never did so or indicated to me any desire not to relate to me.

It is important to add that there were other, younger Kututeng musicians in the outlying villages around the chiefdom capital who played excellently but were not blind. I met and heard one of them but did not have the opportunity to interview or tape-record his music. Peter Davenport, a few years later, met others. And in Bafodea Town and its environs, the area of this study, there were one or two other Kututeng players besides the three I report on here, but they did not play as regularly and were not as well known for their music. I do not think blindness is a typical condition for musicians in Wara Wara Bafodea chiefdom; there were a good number of musicians playing a variety of instruments, mostly in ensembles, and I never met another blind one. Blindness, however, is not rare there. It is caused largely by river- and swamp-borne organisms; eye trouble is often contracted during wet rice farming or the washing of people's bodies and clothes in the streams.

Much of the work of anthropologists has been concerned with the so-called central aspects of culture: politics and power, kinship and family, religion, economics, and law. I myself have written in some of these areas. But I believe it is often equally revealing to write about the supposedly less central features. Music is one — a subject not treated nearly so well by anthropologists in data and theory as are other areas, not only because of the technical knowledge problem it imposes but also because of its supposed lack of centrality to culture. Within the category *music,* I here treat of a somewhat minor musical form, Kututeng. Failures in the farm system and major changes in the political structure, the religious system, and the law have occurred in my research area in recent years and have had profound effects on the society and its culture.

But changes in Kututeng have not caused major transformations in Bafodea society, nor would its disappearance do so. The music would be missed by some and would lead to some reordering of other musical forms and performances, or perhaps to the introduction of new musical instruments, such as the guitar, to replace the kututeng, but its loss would not substantially affect the basic structure of the society and its culture as changes in other areas have done. (However, major changes in a substantial number of musical forms, including Kututeng, in the chiefdom would have an effect, if for no other reason than their ties to ritual forms.) My anthropological colleagues who graze in the "more important" fields of society and culture may wonder what I am doing playing around with kututeng musicians. But I believe it is often the apparently obscure, less immediately noticeable, seemingly less germane aspects of culture, by Western standards, that are the most revealing and reflective, if one avoids searching for exotica for their own sake. If there is value in this study, it lies, paradoxically, in the supposed unimportance of its topic—in some human understanding of three persons whose lives focus our attention on a quiet area in another culture.

Musicians' Life Histories

What other body of research on musician's lives and work by anthropologists, ethnomusicologists, and sociologists exists within which my study can be placed? The ethnomusicologist and anthropologist Bruno Nettl (1983:278) comments that "the literature in the field provides surprisingly little information about the individual in music." Others, he writes (Nettl 1983:278), feel that because the music of those peoples whom ethnomusicologists usually study is highly communal, and because it changes little over time, the study of individual musicians through time is meaningless. To Nettl, as well as myself, these attitudes are clearly false.

In fact, there are a small number of excellent studies to draw upon. For Africa, Merriam's (1964:133-40, 1973, 1977, 1979) analyses of musicians in one small Bala village in Zaire raises the paradoxical issue of their low status and deviant behavior in contrast to their importance in ritual and other activities. He notes that there are limits to how deviant the musicians may be before being punished; an allowable deviance is at work here. Ames (1968, 1973a, 1973b) finds that although the generally hereditary musicians of the centralized Hausa state of Zaria in northern Nigeria have low status, which he considers likely due to Muslim influence, they are sometimes quite wealthy. In a comparison of Hausa musicians with those in Obimo, an Igbo group in southeastern Nigeria, Ames (1973a, 1973b) shows how clearly the social position and activities of musicians are related to the social structure and status system of the society at large, in the process explaining why these Igbo musicians lack low status.

Christopher Waterman's (1990:22) study of contemporary Yoruba *juju* musicians in Nigeria also considers the ambivalent social situation of these popular performers. Hugo Zemp (1967) describes how four West African musicians from four different cultures—Baule, Dan, Senufo, and Malinka—in the Ivory Coast became performers, and he provides other useful data on musicians elsewhere (Zemp 1964, 1971). Charles Keil (1979:97-157) discusses the very creative activities of Tiv song composers in Nigeria, who are perhaps more creative than musicians in some other African societies—or perhaps they appear to be so simply because adequate studies of creativity are often lacking elsewhere. He also comments on the Tiv composers' deviant status (Keil 1979:154). J. H. Kwabena Nketia (1973), referring to Akan musicians in the largely centralized Akan society in Ghana, finds that, like their Hausa counterparts, these musicians are grouped into associations, their opportunities to become musicians are often inherited, and, except for lute and guitar players, their prestige is high. Lute players and guitarists "are associated in the popular mind with excesses, particularly with regard to the taking of alcohol" (Nketia 1973:94), so parents discourage their children from learning these instruments.

For Zimbabwe, Berliner (1978:207-39) describes the lives of seven Shona players of the mbira, a small lamellaphone similar to the kututeng but generally more complex in arrangement. Certain characteristic patterns appear: the association of musicians with ancestors; the importance of dreams in encouraging males to learn the instrument and in stimulating them to create new compositions; the significance of the family in developing musicianship, even to the point where ensembles are composed entirely of relatives; and the fact that most musicians have other jobs besides performing, as well as urban living experiences. The status of mbira musicians in traditional Shona culture is high, although this is not always so among Christianized Shona. Andrew Tracey (1961) describes a little of the life and much of the music of another Shona mbira player from Zimbabwe.

The only autobiography of an African musician that I am familiar with is that of Albert Ssempeke (1975), a Buganda musician who continues to learn to play new instruments without giving up earlier ones, thus, in stepwise fashion, expanding his repertoire. Biographical studies of popular urban African musicians exist as well, including Veit Erlmann's (1991:112–55) biography of the Black South African performer and composer Reuben T. Caluza, and Carlos Moore's (1982) book on Fela Anikulapo-Kuti, a Nigerian musician who was a major influence on the growth of the Afro-beat musical genre. A composer of songs critical of the Nigerian government, he was jailed for his political views. The work is partly autobiography and partly composed of interviews with people who have known Fela, as he is popularly called.

These African studies suggest features of musicians' lives that are of concern to me here: the question of their being considered deviants, the place of musicians in the structure and culture of society, the extent of creativity as opposed to the development of new music from external sources, and questions of training and family influence on musicians.

There are also some excellent life histories from other parts of the world that provide insight into musicians as human beings. Melville Herskovits (1944), my former professor, discusses the training, background, and experience of Afro-Brazilian drummers in Bahian religious cults. Another example is Charlotte Frisbie and

David McAllester's (1978) edited life of a Navajo who specialized in Blessingway songs, a key aspect of certain Navajo rituals. The singer, Frank Mitchell, tells of his life in his own words, recorded by the editors. We see him maturing both in musicality and in leadership over time. Neither role in Navajo culture necessarily presupposes the other, and in ethnomusicological studies it is rare to find an account of a musician who reaches high status as a general leader as well.

Another detailed and humanistically oriented study, that of five Shoshone Indian women (Vander 1988), is remarkable in that the singers range in age from their twenties to their seventies. The author employs these age differences to explore Shoshone musical change during the twentieth century along with changes in social and political conditions on the reservation and the changing influence of other Indians and non-Indians on Shoshones. Vander addresses questions of Shoshone and Indian identity as reflected in song, and one gets a good feel for the personalities of the singers, which are related to their life experiences and their ages. Richard Waterman (1956), discussing the music of the Yirkalla of Australia, shows how, at different stages of Yirkalla life, people learn different musical forms and how these musical experiences, particularly among males, are ways of acquiring knowledge about cultural elements much broader than the music itself.

Turning to studies of Western music relevant to my work, the anthropologist and ethnologist John Blacking (1987), while analyzing the musical ideas of the Western composer Percy Grainger, explores his own concepts of folk music, of music as bodily experience, and of music as the product of intensely personal experience and personality. The anthropologist Ruth Finnegan (1989)—who earlier carried out oral literature studies among the Limba (1967), although not at Wara Wara Bafodea, and who uses much the same general framework of analysis as I do—explores the everyday musical experience and the work and attitudes of amateur musicians in the new English city of Milton Keynes. She argues for the importance of studying local amateur musicians and their performances and audiences rather than simply concentrating on professional musicians, as most Western scholars have done. Her focus, much like mine here, is on the practices of musicians and their followers, not on musical theory and analysis. Finnegan shows the considerable musical creativity and enterprise displayed by these amateurs. She attempts the not-always-easy task of clearly delineating the boundaries between the amateur and the professional musician, a matter of some importance in my work. She also emphasizes the role of the audience in relationship to the musicians, as well as the social organization of musical groups. Her work suggests that while in some sense there is one world of music among amateurs in Milton Keynes, there are, at the same time, plural and largely unrelated amateur musical worlds interlinked by the "pathways," as Finnegan calls them, of some individuals. Pathways are her way of following the musical activities of individual performers and audience members through time—a social network approach to the relationships of people involved with music.

The sociologist Howard Becker's (1966) study of jazz players, largely in the Chicago area, returns us to the matter of deviance. Becker argues that an understanding of the concept of deviance in the musical world, which involves beliefs about jazz and blues musicians, requires a focus not so much on the behavior of these performers as on the rest of society, which applies rules and sanctions to offenders. He writes (1966:9, italics his) that *"social groups create deviance by making the rules whose infraction constitutes deviance,* and by applying these rules to particular people and labelling them outsiders. From this point of view deviance is *not* a quality of the act the person commits, but rather a consequence of the application by others of rules and sanctions to an 'offender.' The deviant is one to whom the label has been successfully applied; deviant behavior is behavior so labelled." His book details the relationships between social groups and the "outsiders," as he calls these musicians. Merriam's (1969) comments, mentioned earlier, on the deviancy of Bala musicians in Zaire reflect a similar approach. He writes (Merriam 1979:10) that because the musician's role "calls for deviant behavior he so behaves and this helps non-musicians to keep the role intact." Deviance is culturally defined and involves role-making by society. It is an escape from boredom: "non-musicians enjoy the deviance of performers vicariously" (Merriam 1979:10).

Bruce MacLeod (1993) discusses club date musicians in the New York City area who play for receptions, weddings, bar mitzvahs, debutante balls, dinner dances, and the like. Performing without sheet music, these "sidepersons," as they are called, do not play "art music," and their sounds are generally backgrounds to other activities. They play the same songs over and over again in different "gigs," often with different musicians. Thus it is not surprising that among musicians they are considered to be of low status, a stigma associated with ideas that they are not good enough to find better kinds of work. In some sense they are considered to be hired servants whose audience is either critical of their work or enthusiastic about it, regardless of how the musicians think they are playing.

Anthropological Life Histories

Because the heart of this book consists of anthropological biographies of three musicians, I want to place my study within the anthropological tradition of life histories, which is a rich and old one, particularly in North America, where it started with students of Franz Boas. The first major anthropological life history was by Paul Radin (1926): the autobiography of a Winnebago Indian as told to Radin (which in fact contains some information on Peyote music). It started a trend that was to involve Margaret Mead, Ruth Benedict, Edward Sapir, and other anthropologists in either life histories or the study of the individual in culture—or in the growing up process, as exemplified by Mead's work in Samoa and New Guinea (1928, 1930). At this early period there were published, among others, the life histories by Ruth Underhill (1936) of a Papago Indian and by Leo Simmons (1942), who edited the autobiography of a Hopi Indian. These kinds of works led into the culture-and-personality approach in anthropology of the 1940s and 1950s and then to less psychologically oriented studies such as Oscar Lewis's *Children of Sanchez* (1961), Sidney Mintz's biography of a poor Puerto Rican man (1960), and Jane Holden Kelley's of a

Yaqui Indian woman (1978), and to further works in the present day.[4]

The life history approach in anthropology has been mainly an American one, focused on American Indians, rather than a British or French scholarly anthropological style. I was a student of Herskovits, who himself took his graduate work with Boas; thus I have some familiarity with the American orientation. In my Igbo research I briefly described the life and work of a Nigerian Igbo carver, Chukwu Okoro (Ottenberg 1975:67-83), and more recently I assisted in the preparation for and publication of an Igbo life history collected and edited by Mary Easterfield (Uku 1993). I have written a number of accounts of my own life as an anthropologist (Ottenberg 1989d, 1990, 1994b). I have also published a book about boys growing up at Afikpo in Igboland (Ottenberg 1989a), which, although not a study of specific individuals in detail, represents collective statements about Afikpo boys' experiences from birth through adolescence. And for some years I have been interviewing Coast Salish Indian visual artists in Washington state and British Columbia and contemporary visual artists in eastern Nigeria, in both cases gathering life histories surrounding their work. All of these experiences except the first occurred after I carried out my Wara Wara Bafodea research and thus have largely been helpful as I retrospectively worked through my data on the Sierra Leone musicians. The role of music in Sierra Leone, however, and the music itself present somewhat different problems in questioning and in analysis than did the other experiences.

Not only has work been done in the American tradition of childhood maturation studies, but there have also been a number of excellent studies of growing up in Africa—for example, those by Lorene Fox (1967), Philip Leis (1972), Christine Oppong (1973), Otto Raum (1940), and Margaret Read (1959). In addition, there are numerous full-life studies in Africa by scholars of varying

4. Langness (1965) provides an excellent survey of the development of life histories in anthropology from the turn of the century to 1965. See also Langness and Frank (1981), which covers some later life histories as well as techniques of life-history research.

backgrounds, the best known probably being that of a Nigerian woman in Hausa country by Mary Smith (1954). Others include four Ugandan lives detailed by Edward Winter (1959), four other African lives in a book edited by Joseph Casagrande (1960), Rwandan biographies set in the historical perspective of that society by Helen Codere (1973), and a study of lives in a Nubian community by John Kennedy (1977). Africans who have written autobiographies include R. Muto Gatheru (1964), Albert Luthali (1962), Dilim Okafor-Omali (1965), and Francis Selormey (1966), and numerous political biographies and autobiographies of Africans are now being published.

These studies of the life histories of musicians and others have helped give me a sense of the importance of time, of personal development and change, and of the unexpected occurrences in the lives of individuals. They have helped me understand how people's creativity in various sectors of experience relate to their personal and cultural surroundings, and how their individual activity influences others and their culture in general terms. The studies provide a rich background to my own work. They suggest that there are many differing ways to approach the life histories and social roles of musicians as performers. Mine is only one—the result of my own background and those of the people of Wara Wara Bafodea, including the musicians, and of the happenstances that led me to northern Sierra Leone, to Bafodea Town, and to these three performers. I claim no expertise in writing life histories; their development during my research was unplanned, although they fitted my move away from the study of social roles and social structure toward a more humanistic and aesthetic view of culture, which in recent years has directed me from the study of kinship and politics to the visual arts and music.

2 The Setting

Little is known of the history of the Limba. Few travellers who have left written records seem to have passed through their country, and British records are generally limited to the period after the declaration of the Protectorate in 1896. —R. H. Finnegan, *Survey of the Limba Peoples of Sierra Leone*

WARA WARA BAFODEA CHIEFDOM, WHICH IN THIS WORK I call by its shorter, popular name, Bafodea, is an ancient Limba chiefdom (Finnegan 1965) located in north-central Sierra Leone (map 1). It is the northernmost and probably the most traditional of seven present-day consolidated Limba chiefdoms in the area (map 2). A look at map 1 suggests that the Limba have either been pressured into smaller areas by cultural groups on their borders or have expanded in three fingerlike directions, or both. Which is the case is uncertain; much of their history is still obscure.

Bafodea lies in beautiful, hilly country with lush, green, well-watered valleys (fig. 1) and rocky cliffs growing out of the valley sides. But it is a poor country by West African standards. It had a single bad road to the outside world at the time of my research, and two new, equally bad roads have been built since then, both for trading what few surplus foods exist. There is little color in the metal-roofed, rectangular houses. Yet the chiefdom has rich and interesting life and music, which is what this book is all about.

The chiefdom stretches some twenty-five miles from its eastern

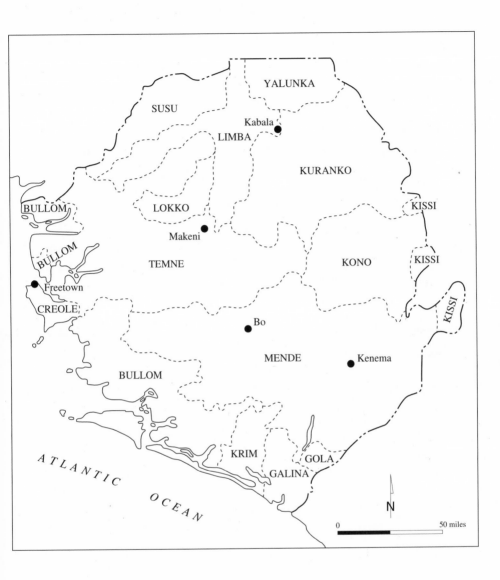

Map 1. *Peoples of Sierra Leone.*

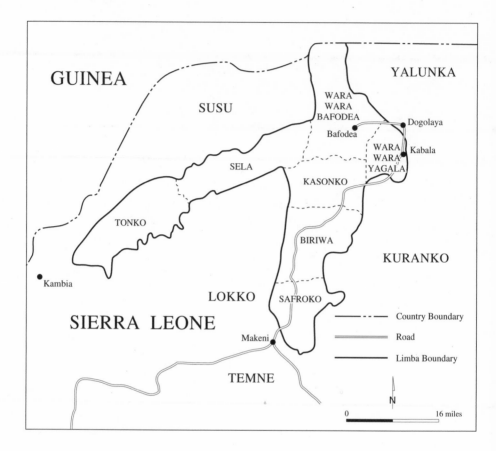

GUINEA

YALUNKA

SUSU

WARA
WARA
BAFODEA

Bafodea ●

● Dogolaya

WARA
WARA
YAGALA

Kabala ●

SELA

KASONKO

TONKO

BIRIWA

KURANKO

● Kambia

LOKKO

SAFROKO

SIERRA LEONE

Makeni ●

TEMNE

	Country Boundary
	Road
	Limba Boundary

N

0   16 miles

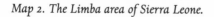

Map 2. The Limba area of Sierra Leone.

border with Wara Wara Yagala, a Limba chiefdom with a culture similar to Bafodea's, to its border with a third Limba chiefdom, Sela, to the west (map 2), beyond which lies the Tonko Limba chiefdom. The northern portions of Bafodea are faced by non-Limba people: the Yalunka to the northeast, the Susu to the northwest, and the Kuranko to the east. At its northernmost, Bafodea reaches the border of Guinea, and a few former Bafodea chiefdom villages lie over this line. To the south lies another Limba chiefdom, Kasonko, and to the southwest live the Lokko people, also known as the Landogo, a non-Limba group (Speed 1991).

Bafodea is the most isolated of all the present-day Limba chiefdoms in Sierra Leone, the least equipped with roads and other forms of communication. It is a colonial-era amalgamation of Bafodea chiefdom in the south and Kamuke chiefdom to its north, both old groupings in the area with no strong histories or myths of migration but with a sense of having been in Sierra Leone longer than the two larger cultural groupings there, the Temne and the Mende to the south. The Bafodea language, part of a non-Mande group, is a Limba dialect that belongs to the West Atlantic language family.

The present combined chiefdom has an area of 372 square miles (Finnegan 1965:11) and a population of some twelve thousand.[1] Its capital, Bafodea Town (fig. 2), where I lived during my research, is a community of some one thousand people at the end of the only two major roads into the chiefdom, both largely dirt and single track, which connect with the Koinadugu District capital of Kabala some fifteen miles to the east. During warfare days, Bafodeans lived mostly in villages on the tops of high hills or in isolated valleys, protected by substantial stone walls and thick thorn bushes. Now they reside largely in open valleys in villages bounded by steep, rocky hills from which flow numerous springs. The country is well-watered as a rule.

In the southern part of the amalgamated chiefdom are found

1. Population figures are from adjusted 1973 returns and from my estimates using census data, both provided by Dr. Armand Thomas, Demographic Unit, Fourah Bay College, Freetown.

Figure 1. A typical view of the Bafodea countryside, looking north from the top of the hill at Bafodea Town. Photograph by Labelle Prussin.

Figure 2. A typical street in Bafodea Town, viewed from my house.

wet rice fields in the soil-rich valleys and stream areas. Dry rice farming and peanut growing take place in the more barren uplands, with some tropical forest growth here and there. Palm wine tapping is a popular activity, particularly in the chiefdom's south, and Limba tappers from Bafodea and elsewhere are well known for their work throughout Sierra Leone—they are sometimes prized for this occupation and at other times denigrated for it. In the north of the chiefdom, the country is savannalike, and millet is the predominant crop. There, Muslim Mandingo farmers and cattle herders exist in small numbers along with the more numerous Limba farmers. Throughout the chiefdom are found Muslim Fula cattle herders, usually in semipermanent settlements, moving their cattle from area to area as the seasons change. Conflicts between Fula herders and Limba farmers over Fula cattle eating Limba crops are common. Wara Ware Bafodea is a chiefdom of both Christians and Muslims in the south and largely of Muslims in the north. Yet most people throughout Bafodea are followers of traditional religion as well, whatever they may call themselves (Ottenberg 1986). They believe in the power of a high god, Kanu, and of the ancestors, and they hold strong witchcraft beliefs; antiwitchcraft activities are endemic.

Social Groupings

Bafodea is dominated by three widely dispersed, exogamous, patrilineal clans: Kamara, Mansaray, and Konteh (sometimes spelled Conteh). It is a small-scale, traditional state with only a few officeholders. The Bafodea Paramount Chief (figs. 3 and 4) has by tradition been a Mansaray through many successions. His assistant, or Speaker (fig. 5), always comes from another clan to create a political balance of sorts. Bafodea is not a highly autocratic, centralized polity, although the chief holds considerable power to try legal cases and settle disputes, and he has nominal control over both the men's and the women's secret societies in the various communities. He is recognized as Paramount Chief by the federal government and holds a government staff of office in a country

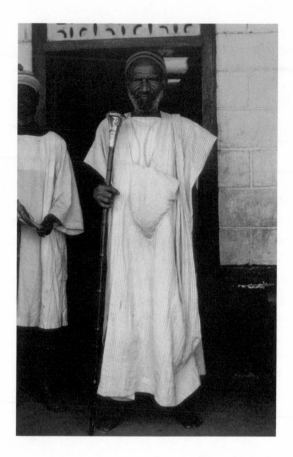

Figure 3. The late Paramount Chief of Bafodea, Alimamy Salifu Mansaray, standing on the porch of his house.

Figure 4. The late Paramount Chief, Alimamy Mansaray (at right), directing communal labor for road building near the village of Kamatentena, not far from Bafodea Town.

Figure 5. The Paramount Chief's Speaker, Pa Hamidu Kamara, on the porch of his house in Bafodea Town.

that still allocates considerable authority to its traditional rulers. Former Bafodea chiefs employed a number of Mandingo or Kuranko xylophone players as musicians who traveled with the chief whenever he moved. The previous and present chiefs were and are nominally Muslim, although they did and still do take part in and uphold most traditional Limba practices.

There are several large towns in the chiefdom in addition to the capital, but most people live in small, scattered villages, and some farmers reside in temporary shelters at their farms for months during the farming period. Villages have considerable autonomy despite the centralized authority in the chiefdom, and village leadership is usually hereditary within the founding clan. A member of one of the other two clans holds the second office, as in the chiefdom center. Travel between communities is largely by foot in this isolated area of Sierra Leone, and even where roads exist there are few vehicles on them.

The main religious mission in the chiefdom is American Wesleyan Methodist; it has been there more than fifty years and operates a primary school in Bafodea Town and several others in villages. Many children, however, receive no Western-style training at all. For secondary school, Kabala is the nearest place to go. Young adults frequently leave Bafodea, disdaining farming as a career, and go to Sierra Leone cities or to the country's diamond fields to the southeast, seeking employment and their fortune. The Sierra Leone army in Freetown has attracted to its ranks a fair number of Bafodea men, accompanied by their families. Despite the chiefdom's isolation—there is no telephone system or wireless, and mail is generally delivered only as far as Kabala—those who leave do keep in touch. They return home for visits and send money back, which is helpful in a chiefdom whose main export is rice and where in some years the harvest has been low or the price farmers received for it has been minimal.

Two-story or otherwise elaborate homes are extremely rare, and material goods, including clothing and furniture, tend to be simple. There is little money to be had except by some wealthy Limba farmers, who rarely display it, keeping their wealth in cattle

held for them by Fula herders. A number of these Fulas are themselves wealthy. Little, if anything, in the way of visual art is seen
when one walks around the villages, either in carvings or wall
murals or in other forms. What visual art exists is rather simple
compared with, say, that of the Mende in southern Sierra Leone
or that in most parts of southern Nigeria (Ottenberg n.d.). The
aesthetic focus is, rather, on music and dance (Ottenberg 1983), in
which there is extensive activity, creativity, and skill.

The Music of Bafodea

Musically, Bafodea is an interethnic blend of genres (Ottenberg
1988b). Although the chiefdom is basically Limba in culture, its
music includes Mandingo and Fula musical forms and ensembles
ultimately deriving from Guinea to the north and from Muslim
Kuranko and Yalunka areas to the east and northeast. From these
external peoples come xylophone traditions and particular forms
of iron gongs, flutes, drums, and rattles. From Limba groups to
the south and west of Bafodea and from the neighboring Lokko
come other instruments and musical forms including the large,
circular bass drum (*huban*), the lamellaphone consisting of a large
wooden box with three metal tongues (*kunkuma*), and the steel or
iron U-bar gong (*kongole*).[2] Christian church music and urban musical traditions derive from Freetown, Makeni, and other urban centers far to the south. Other musical instruments, including wood
idiophones and drum forms, are probably extremely old in the
chiefdom.[3] Although external musical and other influences are felt,
the people of Bafodea retain a strong sense of their own tradition
and identity as Limbas, having lived in their isolated, hilly area for

2. The term *angul* (hard *g*) is also employed at Bafodea and in other parts
of Limba country for the U-bar instrument. Also see Kreutzinger (1966:56),
who indicates that in Freetown the term is employed for the triangle. Van
Oven (1980:fig. 41) refers to it as the *kututor.*

3. Winterbottom (1969 [1803]: 111–13) indicates that a wood ideophone
similar to what I describe as the *nkali* existed in Sierra Leone by 1803, as did
the metal triangle. The U-bar metal idiophone may be a later modification of
the triangle originating in an automobile suspension part.

many centuries with a reputation for being conservative, slow to change, and independent in spirit.

Kututeng music is only part of a larger Bafodea musical scene that includes more than twelve other musical forms, each with its characteristic instruments and sounds and sometimes with a female lead singer. Although the kututeng occasionally appears in an ensemble, Kututeng is the only Bafodea music that is basically a solo form, except for the occasional bamboo flute played casually in a village at night. The remainder of the musical forms are associated with ensembles of two to six players, most often two or three. The dominance of ensemble music at Bafodea is in keeping with much of African music (Nketia 1963:19).

Like most of the other musical forms, Kututeng is played only by males. Whereas other ensembles are hired expressly for major events and rituals, kututeng players rarely are. Instead, they sometimes arrive at events to join the musical scene and the partying; they may pick up a bit of money for their effort in the form of presents from listeners and those who sing in response to their music. Generally, however, they play in the community separately from the hired ensembles. Kututeng music, characteristically, is not directly associated with religious rituals and activities, since its players are not hired for these events and its songs are generally secular. Other musical forms are found in more direct association with second funerals, initiation rites, and the male and female secret societies at Bafodea.

The kututeng is also a quiet instrument. It does not boom out like the drums and wood and iron idiophones frequently played in other Bafodea music, and it is easily drowned out by these other instruments if played at the same time. Its quietness is undoubtedly one reason I was attracted to it. Like other Bafodea music, however, Kututeng has a strong rhythmical and repetitive base, although it is much more melodic than most. It is associated with singing by its instrumentalist and others present, and often with dancing, as is true of most other Bafodea music. Although its players are male, both sexes take part in Kututeng events, as they do in most musical activities at Bafodea except for some gender-related secret society events. Females are very active in singing and dancing at Bafodea, if not always in playing the instruments.

Although I have described some Bafodea instruments and musical forms other than Kututeng elsewhere (Ottenberg 1983:83–88, 1988a, 1988b:452–59, 1989b, 1993), I mention them here briefly to place Kututeng music in the context of the larger musical scene at Bafodea.

Poro music (Ottenberg 1993)—not a form associated with the men's Poro secret societies in other parts of Sierra Leone—includes the wooden idiophone called the *nkali*, also known as a slit gong, which consists of a hollowed-out log with two or three slits on its outside and its ends covered with wood or metal, and which is struck with two wooden sticks (fig. 9). Also in the Poro ensemble is a large bass drum, the huban (fig. 21), and a steel or iron U-bar, the kongole, which is struck with a metal stick (fig. 19). If the kongole is of steel, it often comes from the suspension system of an automobile. Occasionally a kututeng player appears as an addition to the ensemble or as a substitute for the U-bar player. Composed of three or four male musicians, this ensemble plays socially for pleasure and at second funerals and other rites. An ensemble that appears at similar kinds of events and performs similar music to song is the Kunkuma ensemble (Ottenberg 1993), which substitutes the three-tongue wooden box lamellaphone (fig. 19) for the large drum of Poro as a rhythm instrument. The Kunkuma ensemble, too, may occasionally have a kututeng musician join it.

Gbondokali music (Ottenberg 1994a) appears at male adolescent initiations into Gbangbani, the men's secret society, always a major event in Bafodea. It employs the wooden nkali idiophone, long cylindrical drums, or both. Two to four men are the instrumentalists, playing to the boys' acrobatic movements. For the equally important female initiations (Ottenberg 1994a), two to four women play small circular drums placed lengthwise on the ground; this music is quite different from that of the male initiation. In each case, the initiating adolescents dance enthusiastically and at length. The men's secret society makes use of one or more large, wooden, side-blown horns (Hart 1989:50–51, figs. 6–7;

Ottenberg 1994a:375-76) whose sacred sound represents the voice of the society. Gbangbani initiations also employ a number of long, single-grooved, wood idiophones, *huyenki* (Hart 1989:51, figs. 8-9; Ottenberg 1994a:375-76). These two types of instruments are frequently used together for Gbangbani activities, but only in secret in the bush or when, in Bafodea communities, nonmembers of the male secret society remain in their closed and shuttered residences—though the sounds can be heard from some distance by everyone. The women's secret society, Bondo, plays Bondo music at various rites both in and out of the bush, the latter generally open for all to hear and see. A number of females sing while shaking round gourds with networks of strings on their external surfaces, which hold beads of various sorts.

At marriage rites, Gbongbo music is played by one or two men on the nkali as the bride dances in her village before going to the groom's home. Mayoi music is generally played by three or four men using a wood nkali, a small drum, a metal U-bar, and sometimes raffia rattles, often accompanied by a female singer who dances as well. It is found particularly in the northern region of the chiefdom and is played at some second funerals and at work parties. In the chiefdom's southern region, one hears Kukangtan music played for second funerals by two women on drums of the sort employed in the girls' initiation rites, generally with two men playing wood nkali as well. There are also a variety of forms of farm music heard during ground clearing, weeding, and rice threshing. In them, men employ either long cylindrical drums, hour-glass drums, wooden gongs, or some combination of the three. For each of these events, different forms of music are generally performed.

Last, some Mandingo ensembles are found in the chiefdom, as well as an occasional Yalunka group from the northeast and Kuranko ones from the east. These ensembles consist principally of Balanji players performing on xylophones with twelve or more wooden slats, with gourd resonating mechanisms slung underneath the slats (figs. 28, 29). They appear at various Mandingo and Limba traditional rites; often two or three players perform together. Balanji music, always played by men, has a melodic sound, as do Kututeng and the flute at Bafodea. To the best of my knowledge, however, there are no Mandingo *griots* in the chiefdom;[4] they perform a solo music that, if present, might offer a model of musical form to be copied by the kututeng player. Traveling Fula musical groups, the most professional musicians at Bafodea in terms of maintaining an almost full-time commitment to music as an occupation, appear at Fula and Limba events in ensembles of up to six members or so with a variety of drums, one or more wood flutes, and gourd-piece rattles (van Oven 1981:25–26).

Bafodea ensemble music is mostly heard between roughly October and May, which includes the rice harvest period, the dry season, and the beginning of the planting period. It is not heard much during the height of the farming season, when everyone is busy. Solo music, however—Kututeng and flute—is played pretty much year-round.

Kututeng music thus forms only a small part of a much larger corpus of music at Bafodea, in a society with a rich musical tradition. Still, it is not insignificant music and its sound is commonly known in the chiefdom. It is of interest to me partly because it contrasts with the more numerous ensemble musical forms and because its solo and secular qualities lead it to exhibit considerable variation in musical styles. The kututeng is also an imitative instrument; some Kututeng musicians imitate Poro, Kunkuma, Balanji, and other ensemble music on the kututeng quite readily.

I researched Kututeng music primarily in Bafodea's capital town, the one most altered through contemporary social change. Thus I make no claim about how universal its particular features are in the entire chiefdom. Peter Davenport, from his own field research, informs me (personal communication) that there are very skilled, sighted Kututeng players in some of the Bafodea villages— players I did not hear or interview. A closer investigation of traditional Kututeng would require a careful analysis of this village

4. *Griot* is a well-known term in the western Sudan, especially in Mali and Senegal, for a musician who recounts a people's origin myths, history, and genealogies through song, usually playing a stringed instrument, the *kora*.

music rather than town-oriented music and how it relates to the music of the three Kututeng players discussed in this work.

All the instruments I have described are widespread in Sierra Leone. What varies is the nature of the ensembles and the way the instruments are played (Turay 1966; van Oven 1980, 1981, 1982; Sievers 1992). If there is a center for musical activity in the country, it is not in Bafodea chiefdom but farther south. Bafodea is too isolated to play such a role. Rather, it is a musical area that has absorbed influence from most of the cultural groups around it in all directions, except perhaps from the Susu to the northwest (Ottenberg 1988b).

The Kututeng Instrument in the African Context

The Bafodea kututeng is a lamellaphone belonging to a class of plucked idiophones that are found widely in Africa in various forms and shapes. They usually have metal or wood tongues, which are sometimes called keys or prongs in the literature. The tongues are attached to a flat wooden sounding board, and a half gourd or a wooden or metal box resonator is attached below the board (fig. 12). The instrument is small enough to be held easily in the hands. In Sierra Leone, where it is widespread, it characteristically features a metal box resonator, whereas elsewhere in Africa the resonator is usually a gourd or made of wood. The metal form gives the instrument a somewhat sharper sound than does a gourd or wood resonator, which resonates more softly.

This general form of lamellaphone is clearly identified with Bantu-speaking peoples of south-central and eastern Africa, far outside the Limba area in non-Bantu West Africa. In the Bantu areas, the instrument is well established and well described (Kubik 1980a). Its distribution in Zaire, where it is called the *sanza,* has been surveyed by J. S. Laurenty (1962), and Alan Merriam mentions it there as well (1973:252, 1977:815). For Zambia, A. M. Jones (1950:328) discusses this type of instrument, and it has been well studied and recorded in Zimbabwe, particularly by Paul Berliner (1978) among the Shona, by Andrew Tracey (1961, 1970), and by Dumisani Maraire (1990), himself a Shona mbira musician.[5] Pierre Sallée (1980) mentions its presence in Gabon.

For East Africa, Lois Anderson (1980:315) reports that the instrument was imported from Zaire to Uganda in the early to mid-twentieth century and that it is of various sizes. Other reports from East Africa include that of Klaus Wachsmann (1980:137) for Buganda, where the lamellaphone is again a twentieth-century import from Rwanda and Burundi to the southwest and from the Alur peoples to the northwest. Gerhard Kubik (1980a:570, 1980b) notes its presence in Tanzania, and G. Senoga-Zake (1986:160–61) shows that it is widespread there and in Kenya, where it is known by a variety of names.

It is found sporadically in West Africa (King 1980:406), where it is less associated with religious beliefs and rituals than it is in southern Africa, as, for example, among the Shona (Berliner 1978). In West Africa, B. Surugue (1980:523) finds the instrument in Mali among the Songhay at the bend of the Niger River, its northermost reported point known to me. André Schaeffner (1951:52) locates it among the Kissi of Guinea, and it is present in two forms in Upper Volta (Rosellini 1980:459). As we will see later, it is widespread in Sierra Leone. Ruth Stone (1982:89; personal communication) indicates that the lamellaphone is also widespread in Liberia, where the Kpelle call it *gbele*. Johann Büttikofer (1890, vol. 2, p. 336) identifies it among the coastal Kru of Liberia by the turn of the century. A type of instrument similar to the kunkuma—the large wood box lamellaphone at Bafodea—is also found in Liberia, where it is called *konggoma* among the Vai and Kpelle and *bunduma* among the Gola (Stone 1980:717). Stone (personal communication) believes that this larger instrument originated in the Congo area, hence its name. Because the Bafodea name for this large lamellaphone, *kun-*

5. The Shona mbira is the most intensively recorded of this type of lamellaphone. See, for example, in the discography, Berliner (1973, 1977) and Maraire (1971, n.d.).

kuma, is similar to *konggoma,* the Bafodea instrument also likely has a Congo origin, if Stone is correct.

There are early mentions of lamellaphones in Ivory Coast by Thomas Brisley (1909:300–301) and George Montandon (1919:36), and more recent ones for the Baule by Hugo Zemp (1980:433, n.d.*b* [discography]). He has also written of it and recorded it among the Dan in Ivory Coast (Zemp 1971, n.d.*a* [discography]). J. H. Kwabena Nketia (1963:97, 1980:328) notes two forms in Ghana. Darius Thieme (1967:42) also finds two types of this instrument among the Yoruba of southwestern Nigeria, one of which is unusual in having its bamboo tongues inserted directly into the gourd resonator, with no wooden sounding board to hold the tongues. I have already indicated the instrument's presence among the Igbo of southeastern Nigeria. Hugh Goldie (1862:182), in his dictionary of the Efik language of southeastern Nigeria, gives the Efik word for this instrument, suggesting that it was established there by the time his dictionary was published. It has been reported in Cameroon, by Montandon (1919:36–38, 101), for example.

Both the small and the large forms of lamellaphone have been found in the Caribbean, where they undoubtedly arrived through contact with Africa (Cooke 1980:406). David Thompson (1975–76) gives the distribution of the larger form there, and Harold Courlander describes lamellaphones in Cuba (1942:239) and Haiti (1941: 380–81). Montandon (1919:14) notes that they occur in the Antilles and in Brazil.

If the distribution of these lamellaphones is clear, their origins are not, particularly for the smaller varieties such as the Bafodea kututeng. E. M. von Hornbostel (1933:297) thinks the small lamellaphone originated in the northern part of its African area because there is a tendency to employ wood tongues there, while metal is used more in southern Africa. I have not seen wood tongues used in Sierra Leone, however. Kubik (1964:250) believes the small lamellaphone probably originated in central Africa. A. M. Jones (1964) suggests that it shows Indonesian influence or origin, which would make southern or eastern Africa its place of origin on that continent. Though the issue of the instrument's origin is unsettled, it seems unlikely that it originated in West Africa; it probably spread there from central Africa. It is unclear whether the large and small forms of lamellaphones had the same history.

At Bafodea, both forms of lamellaphones are close to the north-western periphery of their geographic distribution in Africa. It is evident that both types arrived in the chiefdom after long, un-known travels and are now well integrated into the Bafodea musi-cal scene.

3 Sayo Kamara

nantukuse kututeng kunanoma manki
When I die, Kututeng music will bury me

MIDDLE-AGED, TALL, OF MEDIUM BUILD, WEARING LOOSE-fitting old clothes (as do some other men in the chiefdom) with a floppy, broad-rimmed hat, Sayo Kamara (fig. 6) shuffles down the street using a wooden walking stick. I was introduced to him in Bafodea Town one day in October 1978, shortly after I had settled in for my research. It was a chance meeting, but I then invited him to come to my house to play that evening, for I knew him to be a musician (*bayeren*). Although blind, Sayo knows the town well, and he sometimes carries his kututeng in front of him as he moves slowly along, perhaps playing it a bit, holding it in front of him.

Later that day he appears, and my assistant, Paul Hamidu, and I guide him to a seat on my small front porch. He shows me his instrument, the first of its kind that I have seen in Bafodea. It consists of a rectangular-shaped resonator made from an old one-gallon tin container with the metal cut out on one large side, which is the top, and replaced with a flat wooden board (fig. 12). To this are attached eleven small iron tongues, the longest one in the center and the others decreasing in size toward both sides. The screw-cap from the original container has been removed from the metal box. There are pebbles in the box, which sound as Sayo shakes it. Holding it on his lap, sometimes with its back against his waist, he plays

44

Figure 6. Sayo Kamara playing his kututeng in Bafodea Town.

with his thumbs toward him at the distant ends of the tongues, as is common in Sierra Leone, with the remaining fingers holding the two edges of the further end. This is not the usual manner of playing in other parts of Africa, where the instrument is generally played from the end nearest the performer, with the thumbs pointing away from him (Berliner 1978; van Oven 1970:23). Sayo Kamara tells me that at home he has several kututengs with different numbers of tongues. As he plays I hear soft, liquid sounds rather than the heavy, rhythmical patterns of most Bafodea instruments.

He plays for a while, pressing his thumbs rapidly against the tongues, generally a single tongue at a time, slipping them off the flattish, worn edges, for this is a plucked instrument (van Oven 1981:12-13, figs. 20-21). Then he stops, asks me my name, and starts playing again, singing in a strong, low, hoarse voice:

simon mandewu

Over and over he sings "hello, Simon" in Limba. Musicians in the chiefdom often do this, I later discover, when they meet a stranger. It is a way of making contact, sometimes preparatory to singing praises of the person, and sometimes in the hope that he will give the musician a present of money.

Then Sayo sings single lines in Limba, sometimes repeated, which Paul Hamidu roughly translates because my Limba is poor. There are references to me, among other comments, as he performs.

The world is not bad
Some have something
And some have more than others
You have to do whatever work you can
No need to be proud
For when we are dead we are all buried in the same place
I was born blind
From what I play I get everything

The kututeng gives me everything
Hello, Simon, hello
Hello, Paul, hello
Some people call me
I like to play
I get everything from it
People invite me to play and then criticize me
But I am above that
Even the White Man knows me to be a musician

There is a powerful underlying pulse to his singing. His thumbs move quickly on the instrument. As he sings, he occasionally shakes it to rattle the pebbles, but I cannot discover in what pattern. A crowd is gathering, some twenty-five boys and girls standing on and outside my rather small porch, a few men sitting on chairs and stools, and some five women standing—mainly neighborhood people. He says he sings and people answer in song. "Do you want that?" he asks in Limba. I answer yes, whatever he is used to doing.

He commences to sing a song without playing his instrument, teaching the audience to respond with specific words, and then he begins to play. Again and again he sings something and they respond, all in Limba. He does not speak English at all. His voice is loud and steady, a characteristic also of ensemble singers at Bafodea and elsewhere in Africa (Nketia 1973:84), who must be heard over the music of percussion instruments, sometimes in order to lead a chorus.

The Limbas should join hands and work together
For we are all Limbas

Then he shifts to other words, repeated for a few minutes:

The people are selling wine
I want a cup to drink

A woman lying with a man, she said
Later the young man decided not to love her
He explained to people that they did not do anything
[I do not understand this last song. Paul Hamidu quickly explains
that it means the woman was just trying to get people to believe
that they were lovers, but they were not.]

I learned to play the piano when I was in my mother's womb

A young man and a lady cover in the same blanket
It always results in losses

I am too new at Bafodea to understand what some of these
songs are about. Paul Hamidu again explains the last one: when a
man loves a married woman and is caught, he has to pay fines to
her husband. I am surprised at the overt sexual nature of some of
the songs in the presence of children, but they take them in with
delight. It is my own childhood experience, a different upbringing
in which sex was rarely discussed except privately among us boys,
that brings about my reaction. After returning to the United States,
I come to realize that, as Alan Merriam (1964:201) puts it, "music
provides situations in which language behavior is freed from the
restraints imposed by normal discourse," and that song texts are a
means of escape and refuge (Merriam 1964:204).

The children and some of the women are responding in song.
After the start they seem to know many of the words without
Sayo's going over them. For each song, I now realize, there are two
phrases—Sayo's and the responders'—but at this time it is too new
to me to write this down accurately. Later I discover that the texts
of the songs and Sayo's way of playing the kututeng are typical of
him: greetings, a bewailing of his misfortunes, and then proverb-
like sayings and songs of lovers, all coming one after the other in
no apparent order, with repetitions. He shows an evident wish to
hold my attention and interest from start to finish, a clear aware-
ness of my presence.

After performing for about an hour, Sayo suddenly says he wants to go, he is tired. I am not sure whether he is really fatigued or is disappointed that I have not so far given him any money. I do not yet know the custom for paying musicians. Perhaps he is not satisfied with the crowd's reaction to his singing. He stands up and sings, playing his instrument:

Dreams are not true
You may have contact with a person in a dream
You would not expect to meet

As he plays, he knocks with the ends of the fingers of his right hand on the side of his musical box, the first time I have noticed him doing this. I give him a "dash" of about a Leone in coins—worth roughly a U.S. dollar at the time in Sierra Leone. I do not yet know what is a big or small payment in Bafodea, and I am a little uneasy, wanting to please him but afraid of overpaying or underpaying by local standards. Then he sings:

Simon, when I start to play, a poor man,
I am always expecting more

I feel that he is disappointed with this sum, yet I am surprised at his openness—in fact, a little offended. But Paul Hamidu says that it is a good dash and this is just Sayo's sense of humor, his way of responding to me. Much later I realize that he is quite poor, that his songs express his considerable needs, and that he takes me for a rich man, which I am by Bafodea standards.

Then he sings in Krio, the common tongue of Sierra Leone's capital, Freetown. Krio is rapidly becoming the unofficial national language of Sierra Leone, spoken by many young and some middle-aged Bafodeans (Fyle and Jones 1980; E. Jones 1968:207–208; Shrimpton 1987). It was formerly considered a dialect, but linguists now conceive of it as a language. It is a composite of English, a number of West African languages, and some Portuguese.

I dun touch am
I dun sok am
I dun lay am
I dun get am
I dun feel am

After each line the crowd responds:

Somebody dun touch am

It is the most rhythmical piece Sayo has played, with a lively beat. There are many more lines — the song is about a woman who was with one man but leaves him and becomes involved with others. Then Sayo walks off with his kututeng, and people disperse. The next morning I travel out of Bafodea Town in my Land Rover and give him a lift to Sakuta, the village where he was born and lives, about five miles to the east. Sakuta is noted for its storytellers, which Sayo himself once was.

Sakuta used to lie in the hills above the present village. The old settlement was of circular huts with thatched roofs, grouped in a number of clearings. The community was encircled by a protecting wall of sticks that in time grew into tall trees, and also by a heavy row of thick thorn bushes around it. After the road to Bafodea Town was built from the district capital of Kabala in the 1950s, the settlement moved to the "line," as people in the chiefdom call the little-used, narrow earthen auto road. The new settlement developed in the common new style — rectangular houses facing both sides of the road, with metal pan roofs and walls often made of mud blocks (fig. 7). There is only an occasional traditional house. The old village is silent now, waiting for archaeologists to come and probe it.

Sayo's Life

Sayo lives in a single room in one of these new-style houses. The room is small, but it is not uncommon for a man at Bafodea to have only one room, if any, to himself. A younger brother who is a trader owns the house; he has a small shop next door. This man's wife feeds Sayo when he is in Sakuta, but he is away much of the time. Another relative, Pati, the wife of Pa Bemba, a prominent man of the chiefdom, now dead, houses and feeds Sayo when he stays in Bafodea Town, which he does frequently. I have the sense that his relatives are much more generous to him than are the relatives of the other two Kututeng musicians profiled in this study. At least, Sayo never complained to me about minimal treatment from them, as the other two did about their families.

Sayo has never been married, he says, and he has no farms. Blind men in the chiefdom are usually single. Because they cannot farm, they cannot support a wife and family and so are unpopular as husbands. Although women shun sightless men as husbands, they seem sometimes to be attracted to their music if the men are performers, and they often sing and clap and dance with them. He is impotent, Sayo says, which came on when blindness set in during his boyhood. Although he sometimes sings that he was born blind, this is more a way of saying that blindness is his fate.

Blindness, *human kothaya* (he or she is blind — eyes), is not rare in the chiefdom, although I have no figures on the number of sightless persons. People of all ages, including small children, go blind from onchocerciasis, a disease caused by a systemic roundworm, *Onchocerca volvulus,* that is transmitted by black flies around the numerous rivers and streams in Bafodea.

Sayo does not know how old he was when he lost his eyesight; as a rule, Bafodeans do not keep track of exact ages. He was a boy, though, circumcised with other teenage lads after becoming blind. Because of his condition, he did not go through the full initiation rites into Gbangbani, the men's secret society, which virtually all males at Bafodea join. Failure to complete the basic initiation cuts one off from a sense of comradeship with males of the same age who have gone through the initiation together; I suspect this affected Sayo.

When he was a boy, Sayo's eyes were disturbing him and he felt pain in them. He was frightened but did not go to a European

Figure 7. Sayo Kamara's village, Sakuta, looking east down the only street that bisects it, the old Kabala-Bafodea Town road.

Figure 8. My field assistant, Paul Hamidu Mansaray, playing a bamboo flute, the kuthoyiya.

doctor; few Bafodeans did then—the nearest one was at Kabala, then thirty miles away by road. He went to a traditional medicine man, who told him there was nothing he could do about it, that his blindness was the work of witches. Sayo believes this. In the chiefdom, witches commonly are thought to harm and kill people as well as to ruin crops, make domestic animals die, and cause other troubles. It is frequently believed that the witch is a close relative of the person attacked or even a friend. The witch attacks aggressively and malevolently by employing spiritual forces under his or her control. Witchcraft beliefs are deeply held, endemic in the area, and a major explanation for most troubles and disasters. Sayo himself did not try to find out who was bewitching him, for he was young then. It should have been the work of his family to do so, he says, but they did not, he knows not why. Other people elaborated on a common Bafodea belief to me: that his blindness was caused by a kind of spider (*wosi*) that enters the body and creates general itchiness and internal irritation. Witches or other evil spirits bring on the spider.

Sayo often sings that it was witches who made him blind. He feels that they did this out of jealousy—that people saw him as a strong boy, serious about work, able to do everything, and this made them spiteful. It is a common Bafodea idea that success creates jealousy, which harms the successful through witchcraft. He does not know how people bewitched him; what is important to him is that it occurred. He actually appears to have very faint vision.

People in Bafodea are sympathetic to blindness. If it is associated with witchcraft matters, it is generally believed not to be the consequence of undesirable behavior on the part of the afflicted person but of others' jealousy, rivalry over something or someone, or simply unknown causes.

Sayo learned to play the kututeng before he went blind. It is an instrument small boys often acquire knowledge of to varying degrees. He has also acquired skill on the wooden nkali idiophone (Lamm 1968:64; Ottenberg 1993; van Oven 1981:22–23, figs. 55, 63) and the side-blown flute with two finger holes, the *kuthothiya*, which is made of bamboo or other material (Lamm 1968:44). These, too, are instruments that boys frequently play, particularly the flute, because it is easy to construct (fig. 8). Much of the melody of the Bafodea flute is similar to that of the kututeng, as are the social settings in which it is played. Paul Berliner's statement (1978:23–24) that "one line of traditional Shona poetry explains that when the Mbira is well played, it sounds like a flute," although made in reference to the Zimbabwe form of kututeng, would not be inappropriate for Bafodea.

After blindness set in, Sayo became serious about the kututeng. He listened to others playing it. He imitated them informally, learning from them, but not, he says, from any single person. Most Bafodea instruments are learned in this way, for there is no formal apprenticeship system for musicians as there is for blacksmiths, and musical skills do not necessarily run in families. Sayo's father was a musician, playing the huban—the large, circular, two-sided drum —in a Poro ensemble (Ottenberg 1993; van Oven 1981:figs. 44, 54), but he did not teach it to Sayo. A younger brother, now dead, sang at rice-threshing time. Sayo claims he is a self-taught musician.

It was not long before I observed that the kututeng is a good instrument for the blind. It is light and easy to carry. It is durable. It can be played any time, not being linked to specific rituals, and whereas most musical ensembles at Bafodea play only in the dry season, the kututeng is played all year long. Because it is generally played alone, the kututeng player has no need to gather other instrumentalists together to perform, though the soloist often draws a small crowd of singers and dancers. It is an instrument, like most at Bafodea, that a blind person can comfortably learn to play: the bodily motions involved are intricate at the finger level but not otherwise.[1] It can be played without anyone's responding other than the musician himself, so he can sing to himself if he feels like doing so, even as he walks. It is an ideal instrument for a lonely person at Bafodea. The player works the tongues and can sing both

---

1. Compare this with Kubik's (1977) account of music and body movements in southeast Angola.

call and response. It is as if two people are talking to each other—a private dialogue. If other people come and listen and join in the singing, then so much the better.

Sayo plays other instruments but claims that he makes most of his musical income from his kututeng and that he likes this work best. If he could make a living from it alone he would do so, he says. He feels that people give him money when he plays because they are sorry for him. I am not certain that he deliberately seeks a sense of sorrow in his music in order to get money from others, but I suspect it because he often sings of his blindness and how witches caused it.

Yet Sayo does not derive much income from his kututeng playing. Rarely is he specifically asked to perform. While I was in the chiefdom, I seem to have been his main patron. The kututeng does not have a mystical origin or history, nor is it associated with the ancestors, in contrast to the Shona mbira (Berliner 1978:49, 51), so it is not in specific demand for most rituals. Kututeng is secular music for amusement and pleasure. Although Samuel Akpabot (1971:63) notes that, contrary to popular belief, such nonritual music is not unusual in Africa, much of the music played at Bafodea occurs in ritual context. At least two ensembles, however, Kunkuma and Poro, are largely secular (Ottenberg 1993).

Sayo often shows up without an explicit invitation at preinitiation rites for boys or girls, at marriages, at second funeral ceremonies, and at villages up to ten miles or so from his home—something that some musical ensembles do as well. His presence is welcome, as a rule, adding to the entertainment at the rite. When he arrives in a community, he carries both his kututeng and small goods to trade, laying the goods out in front of a house. In the evening and at night, he plays voluntarily in front of some house or while walking around the settlement, collecting a crowd of interested children and a few adults. He usually plays only if the main musical group or groups associated with the rite are not performing; if they are, he may perform in a different part of the settlement.

But at such events he gains only a little income from his music

—a few coins offered by pleased listeners or singers, which he may spend partly on drink. One reason he earns little is that the ensembles performing at the rite, being mainly percussion based, play louder and more dramatic forms of music that attract an adult crowd for dancing and singing. Their music, often involving metal and wooden idiophones and drums, can be heard better over the talk of the crowd. Kututeng players at Bafodea seldom play together—there are no ensembles for them, as there are among the Shona of Zimbabwe (Berliner 1978). It is mostly by selling goods and playing instruments other than the kututeng that Sayo makes a small living.

Sayo's Other Musical Activities

From childhood Sayo was a storyteller, having learned from Ku-kuba Konde, a famous performer in his village. But he says he stopped telling tales about five years before I arrived at Bafodea Town; he had lost the knack. People at his sessions ceased to respond to him, though he does not know why. I wonder whether it is part of a general decline in interest in storytelling in the chiefdom or whether it is because Sayo sometimes drinks when he performs and this diminishes his skills. I never heard him tell stories; he did not seem to wish to do so for me.

When he was young, Sayo learned to play the wooden idiophone called nkali by listening to others (Bafodeans place a premium on self-learning). He purchased his nkali with money he earned as a kututeng player. The nkali, slung around the player's neck with cord or cloth strips, is struck at waist or knee height with a wooden stick held in each hand, sometimes covered at the striking end with rubber or cloth (fig. 9). The hollowed-out instrument, with two or three sounding bars that differ in frequency when hit, is the most common instrument in the chiefdom. It is played in a variety of ensembles but rarely by itself.

The first time I ever saw Sayo, he had just arrived in Bafodea Town from Sakuta and was playing an nkali at the Paramount

Chief's house, surrounded by a group of some thirty girls and accompanied by a couple of adolescent boys playing the same type of instrument and a girl blowing an animal's horn. I did not converse with Sayo then but merely watched the group. They had come at the Bafodea chief's request to weed his swamp-rice farms the next day. Sayo was in charge of the group. When working, the weeders respond in song as the musicians play and sing. They are fed by whoever hires them.

Sayo also plays for male work groups who weed or turn the soil for farming. Sometimes he plays with a musician friend, Bambun Konteh, from a village near his own. Bambun, who is not blind, plays a long, thin, single-skin drum, the *kusung,* with his right hand (van Oven 1981:21, fig. 37) and the bivalve iron idiophone *hukenken* (van Oven 1973–74:83, 1981:16–17, fig. 37) at the same time with his left, using an iron thumb ring (fig. 10).[2] This kind of music is known as Mankonkoba. Each member of the male work group, including the musicians, has his farm worked in turn, on which day that person provides food and wine for the group. Girls' weeding groups are often arranged in this way as well. Because Sayo has no farm, he sells his turn to someone else for a few Leones. Sometimes, if a family lacks males for this soil-turning work, girls substitute for them and may accompany the two musicians by singing with them.

In June 1979 I heard Sayo and Bambun play at an upland farm for a group turning over the soil in an area of scattered trees, some already cut down, where rice was to be planted. The music differed from Kututeng, geared as it was to the rhythm of the labor. The workers were arranged in two rows moving uphill toward the musicians as they worked, the musicians occasionally moving backward. Four girls were with this otherwise male group, two of them at a time taking turns singing with Sayo and Bambun as chorus to the musicians' lead, while the other two worked. The

2. The term *hukenken* is from a general Sierra Leone word for this iron idiophone, *ken-ken.*

Figure 9. A work party clearing brush outside of Bafodea Town. Joined by two girl singers, Sayo Kamara (right) plays the wooden nkali *idiophone while Bambun Konteh plays the* kusung *drum and the iron* hukenken *idiophone.*

Figure 10. Bambun Konteh holding an iron hukenken.
He sometimes joins Sayo Kamara in playing for farm clearing work.

laborers did not sing. Sayo, playing the nkali, sang strongly as usual in his hoarse voice. Bambun Konteh, on the drum and iron bivalve idiophone, had a weak voice and sometimes did not sing at all.

s + b   awaye kunegundo kawonkeye yo
          Try quickly, group, the sun has gone
GIRLS   awaye bobwe mynsa manande
          Try, boys, we shall not greet ourselves again
          [not say hello to each other again]

After being repeated numerous times, this song was followed by another:

SAYO   yeyee babena koye
          Yes, I will stand here [play] for you
GIRLS   mayaye ye mayameniye ye owunde kandikoto kusala tunde
          Happy yes, happy yes, my former [a friend I knew before, a male], don't you know that work is very hard?

These are songs to praise and encourage the workers. During the second song, Bambun exhorted the workers, shouting "nyawali nyawali" (you work hard, you work hard), over and over again. Later Sayo sang another line with the same chorus for the girls:

bintoni heye bo bintoni heye kpo
You are wet today, you are wet today, wrong

"Wet" refers to an inactive or stiff body. The song says that they are not working well today, it is not right. Songs urging the workers to work harder and implying that they are lazy are sung routinely, regardless of how well the workers are working.

SAYO   yeeye yo kendibelay sankao
          Yes, yes, lazy man stretching
GIRLS   yeeye wunde bayan dekeyee eyo wundi bayan dekeye

Yes, the one who was for me has gone. Yes, the one who
was for me has gone

Sayo implies to the lazy worker that he is going now, though he
does not leave. The girls say good-bye to the players as if they were
lovers of theirs. Sayo says that this sometimes happens.

SAYO   awaye bobo wo mande keye emoneo
       Lets go, Bobo, I am sexually assertive
GIRLS awaye bobo eyo misa mana nde
       Let's go, Bobo, yes, we will not say hello to each other

Bobo is a generic term for both boys and girls. In this song, a man
is talking to a girl friend. He wants to have sexual intercourse with
her, but she is saying, "No, we will go our way." This is a way of
singing; Sayo is not actually making a sexual advance. While this
is going on, Bambun repeatedly encourages the laborers, saying
"awooye awa keba" (it is nice, try you men [to work]). Later, he
himself takes over the singing of this last song from Sayo.

Upland farming music is a completely different genre from Kututeng music for the lamellaphone. It has its own instruments,
music, and songs having to do with labor and lovers. Sayo says he
knows only seven songs for this type of farm work, but he appears
to enjoy this music. He and Bambun work hard at it but they also
rest a bit; they do not play all the time the laborers are active.
For Sayo, this is another side of his musicianship, one in which he
works with other musicians and his singing is not personalized—
not about his own life and fortunes. Ensembles that perform for
work groups and for the major rites at Bafodea generally have this
impersonal quality in their song texts.

Often when he plays the nkali, Sayo wears a locally made iron
wrist rattle, a *kpeleni*, on the upper side of one or both wrists
(fig. 11). These rattles are one or more inches long and have small
iron balls or pebbles inside them and metal flashlight battery ends
attached to the outside. The kpeleni sounds as Sayo moves his arms
to beat his nkali with both hands. He does not employ them when

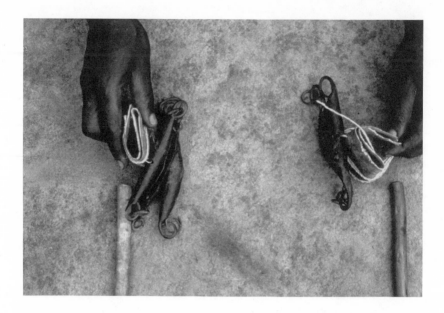

Figure 11. Iron wrist rattles, kpeleni, *tied to leather strips, of the type sometimes worn by Sayo Kamara when he plays the* nkali.

playing the kututeng. In the Mankonkoba ensemble I have just described, the sounds of the wooden nkali, of Sayo's wrist rattles, of Bambun's drum and kukenken, of the voices of the two musicians and the answering girls, and of the pounding of the ground by the hoes all blend with the sound of chirping birds that are attracted by the work and search for food in the cleared areas. The presence of preadolescent and adolescent girls among the men and boys adds interest to the event.

At times Sayo sings alone, without an instrument, at rice threshing on farms. On other occasions in the past he has played his nkali in a Poro ensemble with two other men, one playing the metal U-bar idiophone, the kongole (Ottenberg 1993; van Oven 1981:24, figs. 41, 54), which is struck from side to side with an iron rod, and the other playing the huban drum that Sayo's father also knew how to play.[3] Poro ensembles, playing primarily for pleasure, with singing and dancing, are only occasionally hired for a major rite, though they frequently show up anyway. Their songs are often about love and lovers. Sayo has also played his nkali in a Kukangtan ensemble, joining with a female lead singer who also dances, a second nkali instrumentalist, and two women playing small *samburi* drums. This second funeral music is generally performed at a memorial rite held some years after a person's death. Moreover, Sayo has played his nkali for the boys' preinitiation dance, Gbondokali, along with other musicians on nkali and drums. These musical forms have their own beats and songs.

Thus Sayo has been involved with a number of ensembles, which places him in touch with others in ways he likes. But nowadays he mostly plays the kututeng and the nkali for farm work. He is a musician somewhat in decline, whose career was broader and richer when he was younger. I do not know precisely why he is not employed as much for ensemble work now, except perhaps

3. See Jean Jenkins, "Xylophone Music of the Karanko [*sic*] People" (1979, side B, no. 5 [discography]), for an example of a number of huban drums playing at a Kuranko ceremony with the double iron hukenken and a wooden nkali idiophone, accompanied by a male voice.

that he drinks a good deal and has a reputation for not handling money well in musical groups.

Sayo can still play the bamboo flute, although he rarely does so anymore. When he performs on it, he may attract a crowd that sings with him, often the same single lines he plays with the kututeng, such as

Hand me the beads, let me go with them
[referring to women's waist beads, here a sexual reference]
I am tired, I am tired
Suma, my brother, good-bye
I have come to visit. Hello to Suma

Suma is a popular male name. I was often called Pa Suma, Suma being the Bafodeans' way of saying my first name, Simon, and *pa*, a term of respect for senior Bafodea men, because I had white hair in my beard and on my head and was also often seen as a person of status. I had not thought of myself as old, but I liked the respect that the term conveyed.

Sayo does not play any of the variety of drums and iron idiophones at Bafodea. Yet he is a musician of wide talents, familiar with at least six different genres of music on the nkali. He plays the kututeng and the flute, sings at clearing and threshing events, and has told stories, which often involves singing and nkali performance as well. Although the corpus of music and song for most of these forms of music is not immense, the total range of music that Sayo has played is impressive. Still, he does not play every day or even regularly—unsurprisingly, since there are no full-time Limba musicians in the chiefdom.

Status

Sayo's musicianship does not bring him high status. Blindness itself ensures a low position except when it occurs later in life in prominent senior men. Kututeng playing is often associated with children, for one thing, and Sayo is also poor, wifeless, and farmless.

Other musicians, too, regardless of their instruments, and even if they are fortunate in having sight and a family and farms, have relatively low status, although their skills are recognized and appreciated and they are paid for their work. Because musicians praise people in their songs and depend on presents from those they praise, there is a sense that they are beggars of sorts, a phenomenon Christopher Waterman (1990:22) notes for contemporary juju musicians in Nigeria and that David Ames (1973a:271) notes for Hausa performers. In Bafodea chiefdom, status comes from farming or extensive trading and from turning economic success into large families and success in politics and adjudicating disputes. Being a musician pulls one away from these activities and in some Bafodea minds is associated with drinking and sexual activity. Hard-working farmers go to bed early with their wives, but musicians and others stay up late with women and girls about. "Big men" in the chiefdom hire musicians for events and rites and may have their favorite ones, but even the Paramount Chief today does not have his own personal musicians.

Early in my stay at Bafodea I had, at various times, invited Sayo and other musicians to play on the porch of my house and of course paid them when they did so. This led to annoyance toward me and anger on the part of some elders and big men of Bafodea Town, for I was trying to avoid paying for information when I talked to them. I distinguished between paying for a performance and paying for talk. It is not a distinction Bafodeans make. When one goes to any of them, and certainly to elders and other prominent persons, for assistance of any kind, one is expected to "dash" them (as they say in English-speaking West Africa), no matter what the purpose is. I surmise that they were angered that I was giving money not to them but to people they considered to be of considerably lower status than themselves. In the end, I had to give in because these men, almost as a group, refused to work with me further until I did. After I did so, I had little difficulty.

Money is extremely important at Bafodea, both practically and symbolically. Few social relationships go on for long without the passage of money or kola nuts or some other item. Since musicians are no exception, this practice places their relationships well within the mainstream of Bafodea social behavior.

That prominent persons thought of musicians as being of much lower status led me to begin to reflect on and inquire about the status of musical performers. It is clear that even among musicians, those who play Kututeng music are generally of lower status, for they are hired rarely, if at all, for ensemble work, and their following or audience often consists mainly of children. Ensemble players have a largely adult audience and are often hired to perform. Further, the kututeng is an instrument that children often learn, whereas some other instruments are more adult oriented. The cumulation of factors—blindness, being a musician, and being lower in status than other musicians—places the three musicians I studied low on the social scale, despite the evident enjoyment some people derived from their performances. Yet the fact that all three men are active, playing music and sometimes doing other things rather than simply remaining at home, makes them the subject of some admiration and probably does raise their status a little.

Trading

As for Sayo's other major activity—trading—Paul Hamidu, Fatamata (my other field aide), and I often joked about how often, while driving, we met Sayo on the road outside Bafodea Town on his way to or from the town or Sakuta, his home, or Kasapena, Kandankan, or other settlements in the area to trade and play, often for some rite. We would stop and talk as he held his trade goods, wrapped in cloth, over his shoulder. The package often contained women's head ties, kola nuts, bags of salt, small packets of hair lice power, and secondhand clothes from the United States, along with Sayo's kututeng. Or we would find him on the road, going to or returning from Dogolaya, a Sunday market in the Yalunka chiefdom of Musaia, eighteen miles east of Bafodea Town. There or at the city of Kabala some ten miles south of Dogolaya, he purchased goods to sell.

At one time Sayo was a buying agent for a Lebanese woman trader living at Kabala. Purchasing rice and other foodstuffs, he worked out of Kasapena, a village north of his home, but eventually the arrangement did not work out. He never seemed to make much from his trading in small quantities of goods. Other traders following the same routes to and from village rites moved their goods by truck or hired helpers to headload their supplies, and they carried more and fancier items than did Sayo, who generally moved alone and by foot. Children sometimes stole his goods and his money—he complained that even adults stole money. He was often bothered by thefts, he complained, but whether this was indeed so I could not tell, for he enjoyed appealing to my sympathy in talk as well as in song.

He started trading about 1970, he says, but I believe it was longer ago than that. He has no booth or stand but simply lays his articles out on the porch of a house or on the ground in front of it, perhaps selling a Leone's worth of goods or so in a day. I know of no other trader who plays the kututeng at village events such as marriages, second funerals, or initiations; trading and playing are not necessarily associated at Bafodea. For Sayo, they are tied to his roaming from community to community in search of an income. Twice he "dashed" me a cock, once for rides I had given him that helped him in his trade, and the second time, I believe, for the music I had asked him to play a number of times at my home. I became a casual friend and patron of his.

Dependent on friends and relatives for food and lodging, Sayo is constantly on the move, never staying more than a few days or a week or so in one place. He travels during the rains as well as in the dry season, a perpetual salesman and wandering musician. At village rites he enjoys hearing the music of others, Fula as well as Limba (Fula musicians are sometimes hired for or simply come to Limba festivities), but he says he has not heard the music of the neighboring Yalunka or Kuranko. Communities in the southern part of Bafodea chiefdom are his place of music and trade. He does not play as he travels between villages—this is not a style found among Bafodea kututeng players, as it appears to be among the Lokko to the southwest (John 1952:1045) — although Sayo occasionally plays as he walks about a settlement.

Sayo's Kututeng Instruments

Sayo has two kututengs, and not more, as he once suggested to me. One, purchased some years ago at Kabala, has thirteen flat metal tongues (fig. 12). The other is a nine-tongue instrument bought from a man in Kakoya village, not far from Sayo's home. The smaller one is roughly ten inches long, five inches wide, and four inches high, the other a bit larger. They are typical of others I have seen at Bafodea in appearance and construction, except that the metal buzzer projections at their front ends have disappeared and not been replaced. The instruments are undecorated, unlike some in other parts of Africa (Soderberg 1972). With the exception of carving or incising on some wooden idiophones and wooden horns, Bafodea instruments are not generally embellished with designs. The kututengs are not particularly attractive to the eye, as are the long skin drums (*kusung*) or the xylophones (*balanji*) played in the chiefdom; the metal looks worn and beaten and the instrument is unpolished. The parallel tongues, increasing in length toward the center, form an interesting near-symmetry, but no effort goes into making it an especially attractive instrument visually. Perhaps this is because its box is of metal: the decorated kututeng-like lamellaphones found elsewhere in Africa are generally of wood (Soderberg 1972), on which it is easier to place designs. In Bafodea, the emphasis is on the music that comes from the kututeng, not on its appearance.

The kututeng generally has a one-gallon tin or a like container as a resonator — sometimes a United States AID can for corn or soybean oil — with its screw top gone and one flat side cut away and replaced by a wooden sounding board, the *kurampa*. The board holds the tongues, which are often fashioned by a blacksmith from umbrella stays. The metal box contains pebbles (*pasa*). The instrument usually has a wooden tip projecting out beyond the center of

Figure 12. Sayo Kamara's thirteen-tongue kututeng, with the playing end toward the top of the photograph. Note that the lengths of the tongues at the back end do not correspond to those at the front.

its far end, in the shape of an oval, a rectangle, or a point, of the same thickness as the board itself. On the top side of this projection, a flat piece of metal is often nailed to the wood, its tip projecting beyond the wood extension. To the metal are added, through holes along its edges, bits of coiled wire, battery ends, and other small metal objects. The whole piece, or buzzer, is called *wesewese* at Bafodea, a term that sounds humorous to me but not particularly so to Bafodeans. It makes a buzzing or jingling sound when the instrument is played or shaken, which is much liked by players and listeners.

Whereas Kututeng music and its instrument are called by the same name at Bafodea, the player is called *bayeren*. Among the Temne and Kono peoples of Sierra Leone, the instrument is called *kondi*, which is also its Krio and general name in Sierra Leone (Lamm 1968:65–66; van Oven 1973–74:77–78, 1981:12; Sievers 1992:123–43).

Each tongue (*huteyi*) of the kututeng is of a different pitch. On Sayo's instruments, the tongues are arranged—as is usual in the kututengs I have observed in the chiefdom—so that the shortest one, with the highest frequency, is at the outside right of the instrument as it is held for playing. The next shortest and highest is at the outside left, the third highest is second from the right, the fourth is second from the left, and so on (figs. 12, 15). The center tongue is longest and lowest in sound. This arrangement agrees with that described by van Oven (1962, 1973–74:83) and Sievers (1992:123–43) for Sierra Leone in general. Although A. M. Jones (1950:328), writing of the shaping of the tongues for this instrument among the Lala of Zambia, says that "to produce a low note you need to beat the metal prong wide and thin; for a high note, it needs to be thick and narrow," the tongues of Bafodea kututengs tend to be narrow and flat. Pitch adjustments are made by lengthening the playing ends of the tongues.

Each of Sayo's instruments has three crossbars (*huwe*) holding the tongues. The center one, the restraining bar, is attached to the sounding board with wire and passes across the tops of the tongues, near their centers, holding them down to the board. The other two, the front bridge and the back bridge, are set tightly on either side of the restraining bar, running below the tongues—that is, between them and the sounding board. In one instrument at Bafodea, a third one was added toward the player's body side to firm up the tongues. The two bridges are themselves held in place partly by the pressure of the tongues upon them. The nonplaying ends of the tongues are often irregular in length, which does not seem to affect the tuning because they are not in the vibrating part. The tongues are curled up a bit, especially the nonplaying ends. Sometimes Sayo places a pebble under a tongue behind the back bridge to keep the tongue steady if it is a bit loose in its attachment.

Sayo says he can play the same music and songs with both of his instruments. One time I heard him play his thirteen-tongue instrument using only eleven of its tongues, and another time he played only eight tongues on his nine-tongue kututeng, because the tongues loosen and sometimes become lost or need reattachment.

Each instrument has a hole (*mata*) in the metal box at midpoint on each side to aid in resonating (along with the hole at the far end where the screw cap of the original metal container had been), but there is no hole at the end nearest the player, perhaps because this end is often held against the player's stomach. In some parts of Africa (Kauffman et al. 1980; Trowell and Wachsmann 1953:328), one of these holes is stopped and opened by a finger to change the instrument's sound; this is not done at Bafodea.

Performance

Sayo's musical sounds are a product of the kututeng's tongues, the pebbles in its box as he shakes it, his occasional knocking of the instrument's metal side with the fingers of his right hand, and his singing. Often his sounds are accompanied by the singing and clapping (*ahori*) of those who respond to him, and sometimes by the sounds of dancers' feet on the ground. For other kututengs, there are the sounds of the buzzer, or wesewese, as well. Kututeng music, then, can involve up to seven sound sources, excluding the foot sounds, which are not considered music (*yakali*) at Bafodea as the other sound sources are. Rarely are the instrument's tongues simply played alone. Although they are the focus of the music, along with the instrumentalist's voice, their sounds exist in the context of all the others, a complex and varied arrangement.

The effect is to create sounds as if an ensemble were playing rather than a single instrument—not surprising in a society much of whose music is ensemble work. Indeed, Kututeng is like a mixed ensemble that stresses both the melodic line (definite pitch) through the instrument and voice, and percussion (indefinite pitch) through some of the other sounds (Nketia 1974:112-15). This music differs from that of most Limba ensembles at Bafodea (but not Fula or Mandingo ones) in that the instruments in most Limba music are mainly or entirely percussive and the melodic line is generally produced by the voice alone. I believe that something in the ensemble quality of a Kututeng performance replaces the sense of loneliness of blind musicians like Sayo with a temporary sense of community.

Nketia (1963:99) suggests that much of Ghanaian music employs quick tempo, notes of short duration, and intensity differences. The same appears to be true of much of Kututeng instrumental playing, although the songs appear often to involve notes of longish duration, with few intensity differences. According to Davenport (1984:23, 154, 171-85), almost all the Kututeng music of the three musicians discussed in this book employs the pentatonic scale; only occasionally does Sayo use a hexatonic form (see also van Oven 1981:12-13).

Van Oven (1970:71), in writing of Sierra Leone music, says that "the purpose of the handclaps, one feels, is not to indicate beats but simply to divide time into equal stretches. They will go on steadily even through spoken sections of song." She believes that the free rhythm of the singing is set against this strict time division, and when the soloist sings with a chorus there are often, but not always, considerable differences between their rhythms. The soloist's rhythm may be a good deal freer than that of the chorus (A. M. Jones 1954:28; Merriam 1962:126).

I believe these comments apply well to Kututeng musical performances at Bafodea. The clapping provides a steady time interval around which the kututeng player sings and plays, violating it as he will, but the chorus members' singing is very much integrated with their clapping. The clapping is a frame, a guideline, around which the kututeng player romps, whether he is singing, talking, just playing, or pausing. Clapping adds to the sense of musical community for everyone present without denying the kututeng player his freedom. Merriam (1962) feels that the importance of handclapping in African music has been greatly underestimated in favor of drumming. He writes: "If any single percussion device were to be singled out as most universally used in Africa, we should certainly have to point to handclapping, which is found both where drums are used and where they are not used" (Merriam 1962:121).

All Kututeng players whom I have known at Bafodea have been males; its instrument is considered to be for them (Ottenberg 1983). At performances, however, girls and women form an important part of the singing and clapping: they usually make up the majority of the responders to the instrumentalist. Performances, including Sayo's, may last four hours or more. The adult and child singers and clappers, who are not paid but simply enjoy taking part, arrive and leave as they wish.

Sayo sits on a chair, a stool, or a bed, holding the kututeng in his lap, sometimes with its back against his waist (van Oven 1970:22 [photo]). He does not sit very low or lay the kututeng on the floor to play, as some other musicians do. When warmed up, he may stand and hop about to his own rhythm and singing, holding the instrument in front of him with his body bent forward a bit, turned to the person to whom he is singing, for he clearly recognizes voices. He plays with his thumbs, normally one at a time rather than both together as some others do (Davenport 1984:156–57). He shakes the box, sings, and plays. The pebbles rattle, and he occasionally knocks the box with his righthand fingers. Unless he is in an enclosed room, which is rare, a crowd of children of both sexes soon gathers, along with some adult men and women. They sing in response, Sayo indicating words to them if they do not know them, and they clap and sometimes also dance. Usually no one among them leads, although sometimes a woman plays a guiding role in singing and clapping.

The children, and sometimes the adults, talk a lot as Sayo plays, as is the case for other music in the chiefdom. Bafodeans do not share the Euro-American sense that there should be silence during certain kinds of performances. Nor does their clapping when a piece is over indicate approval, although someone may say "ayoho" (fine) or something like that. The background noise of the talking crowd is a constant problem in making recordings but in fact is part of the total performance. Bafodeans do not seem comfortable remaining totally quiet at musical events. The noise, which adds a sense of excitement and community, is an aspect of Bafodean musical aesthetics (Nketia 1974:239). Once, after being at Bafodea for some time, I recorded a kututeng player, deliberately excluding the sounds of other people to improve the recording quality. But I felt that something important was missing. The absence of responders and perhaps of background talk led to a failure of proper stimulation for the musician.

Bafodeans use the term *bameyni,* which I translate as "responders" or "chorus," for people at any musical event who respond to music by singing. Clearly they are integral to the performances; their clapping (Chernoff 1979:33n19) and singing are essential. They are neither an audience in our Western sense nor just listeners. When I use the term *chorus,* it does not imply a well-organized group but, at Bafodea, an informal gathering of people. Kututeng performances mainly involve children, who are attracted to the music. John Chernoff writes (1979:50): "In African music it is the listener or dancer who has to supply the beat; the listener must be *actively engaged* in making sense of the music, the music itself does not become the concentrated focus of the event, as at a concert" (italics his).

Sometimes Sayo stops to rest for a few minutes, to drink some palm wine or native gin or to make and smoke a cigarette. He may pause between pieces or go directly from one to another; there appears to be no pattern—it depends on how he feels. He may play for three or four hours or just for a short period. Whereas ensemble music for major rites often goes on throughout the night, with rest periods, kututeng musicians rarely play late, probably because the player has not been specifically hired and toward a late hour is unlikely to receive any more presents for his music.

ˋSayo is comfortable with his instrument and his singing; he enjoys playing. Only occasionally does he become irritable when the responders do not reply well with song, when he is unable to attract a good-sized group, or when he derives little or no money from his playing. Like most Bafodea musicians, he is sensitive about being paid, not only because he needs the money but also because it is a sign of recognition. Since he is rarely hired to play Kututeng music, he is dependent on gifts. On Christmas Day, 1980, I observed Sayo walking about Bafodea Town playing, stopping to perform outside some houses, and making about a Leone. But I have also seen him play and move about at rites where no one paid attention to him. I paid him rather more than others would in the chiefdom; some of this he used to increase his trading supplies, and some he used to buy food and drink.

Sometimes after recording Sayo with my rather elaborate (to me) two-microphone Stellavox machine, I would play some of the tape back to him. He enjoyed this immensely, although he commented little on his music. He is not a musician with an extensive vocabulary to describe his playing or his kinds of music. He sees himself as just a player, so I did not expect much comment from him. But I was not the only person in the chiefdom with a tape recorder. A number of men, often traders or teachers, own cassette recorders and enjoy taping traditional music, which they later play for pleasure or take to urban areas where they work and have homes, to play for others from Bafodea. Sayo, like other musicians, is occasionally involved with some of these people.

Once, on the second day of a three-day final initiation rite for girls in his home village, I found Sayo sitting on the bed in his simply furnished room, playing the kututeng and singing as five male friends listened. One of them from Bafodea Town, a lorry driver for a large store in Freetown, was taping him. Sayo played freely, and then the man asked him to play Warana, a kind of music without song to which people dance. Afterward, the friend played the Warana tape back loudly—louder than Sayo's playing—saying in Krio, "Mi broders na Friton de gon lek dis!" (my brothers in Freetown will like this). They will also dance to it, he added. Sayo, excited by his own Warana music, got up and moved about with the strong foot stamping characteristic of this dance: he was very happy.

At the time, Sayo was also selling a few old clothes from a table set out in front of his house, and some kola nuts on the porch floor. He told me he was helping his younger brother put two daughters through the initiation rite and that any money I gave him would be passed on to this brother. I dashed him two Leones, and later he gave me a chicken to feed myself. Because I was a visitor to his town for a major rite to which he had previously invited me, this was an expected exchange. Earlier in the day—on the advice of a Yalunka diviner in Kamasiri, a village on Sayo's route to Dogolaya market—Sayo had done a sacrifice for himself in his room, letting the chicken go free as is sometimes done. "For the sake of the Lord, for good health," he said. Having no family of his own, he maintains contact with his two younger brothers, although I perceive him as a person without close kin ties in a world where these are endemic. Marriage and children make the difference; blindness has social consequences at Bafodea.

A little later I heard the same Warana music being played at a small shop across the street where, the night before, Highlife, Reggae, and other contemporary music emanated from a cassette recorder. I went over and found Sayo, very pleased, listening to his performance as some boys danced to it on the porch. Then Sayo joined in, happy to be moving to his own music, dancing enthusiastically, arms swinging about. The next day I heard the same tape and other forms of music at this store, with boys dancing, but I did not see Sayo. No one thinks it odd for a musician to move from one musical genre to another, from the traditional to the contemporary and back again. Only the anthropologist, with his or her penchant for classifying, seems struck by this. Other music connected with the girls' initiation was being played on these days as well.

One time, after I had been at Bafodea Town for about nine months, I gave an afternoon feast of goat meat, sauce, and rice for the town elders and my friends. In the evening, Muctaru Mansaray, another Kututeng musician, came to my porch to greet me. He felt happy about the meal, he said, to which he had been invited and had come. Then he sat down and played and sang strongly, soon attracting a crowd of children between roughly four and ten years of age, who gradually began to clap and then sing in response to his playing. Sayo, attracted by the music, came with his own instrument and sat on the porch and listened, soon quietly following Muctaru's playing on his own kututeng. When Muctaru stopped for a moment, Sayo broke into song even more loudly than Muctaru and played his instrument, the children responding in song. Then Muctaru began to play again, now following Sayo, who dominated him musically. This was the only time I heard two kututeng players together at Bafodea—a rare occurrence. They continued until a musical ensemble I had hired for the night came, when I had them stop.

This event suggests rivalry or competition, gently handled, something characteristic of relationships among a number of musicians on various instruments in the chiefdom in terms of attracting a following, getting asked to play at major rites, and receiving decent payment. Sayo says he occasionally plays with another Kututeng musician, Marehu Mansaray, who on those occasions plays the other form of lamellaphone, the large wooden kunkuma with its three metal tongues (van Oven 1981:13–14). I never heard them do this, however, nor did Marehu ever mention it to me. These three musicians—Sayo, Marehu, and Muctaru—are the three principal adult kututeng performers in the Bafodea Town area.

The songs that Sayo sings are not secondary to the playing of his instrument. They are an integral part of his performance—powerful, interesting, asking for vocal response and clapping from those present. As a rule, he does not sing without playing, but he may play for short periods without singing, or he may play music that lacks a vocal component, such as Warana. But most often he plays and sings together or alternates short phrases of each. When Sayo plays and sings alone or with just a few other people, it is clear that a dialogue is going on between his fingers and his mouth. Sometimes it is started by the instrument, sometimes by voice and instrument together, and occasionally by the voice alone. The kututeng is usually positioned so that the resonator reflects directly back to the player's face; he hears his music best of all (Berliner 1978:127). This dialogue is a good discourse for a blind and sometimes lonely man. Even when he has a full group clapping and responding to his performance, one has a sense that Sayo is communicating with himself—that he is enveloped in his own person—more so than Marehu or Muctaru.

Sayo's Song Types

Liking to classify matters in my anthropological way, I tried to get Sayo to name and categorize his forms of music, but this attempt at Western scholarly order largely failed. Sayo says he has no names for particular songs that he sings, nor does the chorus. Songs are identified by their first line or a phrase from it, or by the response of the chorus—usually a single line. Call-and-response music, of course, is common in Africa (Nketia 1974:140–43); it certainly occurs in many Bafodea musical forms. Either Sayo sings a first line and the responders know what to sing, or else he sings both the first and the chorus line so that the responders know how to reply. I judge that most songs he sings are already known by the chorus. Later I discuss Sayo's own simple breakdown of his music.

Upon my return from the field, I opted for classification and divided Sayo's song texts into three types labeled I, II, and III, based on their structure but not their content.[4] Regardless of classifica-

4. I employ song text rather than vocal or instrumental qualities as the basis for my classification because of my own musical limitations: I can perceive differences in song texts more readily than in other features. See Nketia (1974:chapter 13) for various types of vocal arrangements in African music,

tion, the songs are usually repeated again and again. They generally are either personal or social commentaries, but they do not
build up into a lengthy tale or history.

Type I Songs

In type I songs, with which Sayo often begins a performance, he
sings a line while playing his instrument, and the chorus responds
with a second line as he continues to play without singing. Sayo
then goes to a new line, but the chorus responds again with its
original line and continues to do so as he sings additional new
lines, as he repeats a line he has already sung one or more times,
or as he returns to a line later. The contents of his own lines may
or may not be connected to one another; often they are not, or at
least not obviously. Rather than telling a long story, the song texts
invoke certain moods, and certain subjects appear repeatedly—
forms of greeting, Sayo's personal misfortunes, witchcraft, matters
of love and lovers, and death.

For one performance at my house, a taping session arranged
almost a year after we had met, Sayo comes to my porch, where a
crowd has been attracted largely by his presence. We greet, and he
sits down. He is quiet for a moment and then says he is blind and
that when he comes to play, if people do not give him something,
he stops. I take this to mean that he wants a dash, but perhaps he is
suggesting the usual etiquette practiced in hiring musicians, which
is first to give them kola nuts or the equivalent in cash—some fifty
cents—when arranging for them to play (which I did not do), and
then some kola nuts and wine when they arrive (which I also had
not done), and then a final payment at or toward the end of the
performance. I respond by saying that I will pay him at the end
(American style?), and he seems reassured by this stranger who
does not yet seem to know the proper procedure. Clearly, he is re-
minding me of his role as a musician. Why did I not follow the

Nketia (1963:28-31) for song types in Ghana, and van Oven (1981:30-50) for
those in Sierra Leone.

accepted procedure? I do not know, except that I was still firmly embedded in my own culture's contractual procedures, and I often found the phrasing of almost every social relationship at Bafodea in financial terms to be irritating.

Sayo begins by playing for a few minutes on his instrument without singing, a form of Kututeng that other kututeng instrumentalists call Tenkele (Davenport 1984:57–64). This prelude is characteristic of Kututeng but does not resemble the melodies that are to come. It is, I believe, a very traditional form of Kututeng music. Peter Davenport (1984:60) describes it as including, among other features, "(1) rapid 'ornamental' trill-like figures, (2) quick runs of notes in scalar patterns, descending and ascending, (3) sequences of three-note descents or ascents." The sound of Tenkele attracts people to the Kututeng music, a sign that it is beginning.

Sayo's first song lines are usually greetings, as is often true for other musicians at Bafodea. The chorus knows the song and goes into its response without being told. He plays his instrument throughout all the singing here.

SAYO   koyama eyooo mande yanke
CHORUS   koyama

Koyama has no specific meaning to Sayo. In going over the tape with him later, he could not explain it, nor could I, although it is phonetically acceptable as Limba. There are sometimes words like this in Limba songs. The rest of his phrase means, "Yes, I have gone." I ask him why he sings this, since he has just arrived! He says there is no reason—he just started with the song. This may suggest that I am paying too much attention to the words when it is the act of singing that is important. To me, however, this phrase refers to a change of place; it is another way of saying that he has come, that he has moved from one situation to another. Perhaps it also indicates some anxiety about playing for me and my tape recorder, an unconscious wish to leave, although Sayo seems anything but anxious.

SAYO   eyo mande beka
          Yes, Mande [here a woman's name; no particular
          person is meant], it is not bad
CHORUS   koyama
SAYO   eyo manke mina
          Yes, Manke [man's name], we are related
CHORUS   koyama

Sayo then sings this line using other names, referring to other people. Then he goes on:

SAYO   mande, suma mande
          Hello, Simon [referring to me], hello
CHORUS   koyama
SAYO   suma beka, suma mande, suma beka
          Suma, how are you? Suma, hello, Suma, how are you?
CHORUS   koyama
SAYO   ansebedi, maneyane
          I am afraid because the Lord has made me so
          [referring to his eyes]
CHORUS   koyame
SAYO   suma beka, suma mande
CHORUS   koyama

He repeats earlier phrases he has sung, and after each line the chorus responds with *koyama*. Then he sings a series of lines before indicating by a pause that the chorus should come in.

SAYO   eyoo titi mina
          mande suma mande, a tenka mane
          eyoo suma, beka
          ansebedi maneyane
          Yes, Titi [girl's name], we are related
          Hello, Simon, hello, I've come to greet you
          I am afraid because the Lord made me so [blind]

CHORUS   koyama
SAYO   kunama, ya mankua
          They will bury me with it
          [they will play Kututeng at my funeral]
CHORUS   koyama

Then he repeats his last line and the chorus sings its line, but sub-stitutes "kututeng" for "it." This is followed by repeats of earlier phrases, and then:

SAYO   kunama ya dagina
          They will lay me on it [his instrument will be his
          stretcher to carry him to the graveyard at his burial]
CHORUS   koyama
SAYO   suma mande
          Suma, hello
CHORUS   koyama
SAYO   toro bene ba kini
          Struggle, people who give birth
CHORUS   koyama

He is happy for people who give birth. He has no children of his own.

Now he goes over earlier verses again, sometimes repeating the same line two or three times before the chorus joins in. He has a particular way of pausing that tells the chorus when to enter. Then he breaks off.

This, then, is the pattern of one of Sayo's types of singing: it has a set chorus line, usually shorter or at least not longer than his own line. He may employ one chorus line for fifteen minutes or so, then stop and have the chorus sing a new line for a while, then a third, and so on, even going back to an earlier one. Or he may go to a different type of singing altogether. In this type I song, he may employ the same lead lines to different chorus lines, sung in different songs, so that his lines do not have to go together with those of the chorus. This suggests that the act of singing, along with general content and mood setting, is more important than specific communication. Some of the lines Sayo and the chorus sing in these type I songs are also sung in Kunkuma and Poro ensemble music (Ottenberg 1993).

At times he varies this pattern by adding an afterphrase, following the chorus's line. For example:

SAYO   awaye sayo awa, kunko nono yan bakaye sayundo,
          kunko nono yan boka
          Let's go, Sayo, let's go. They will bury me with it,
          Sayo, they will bury me with it
CHORUS awaye, sayo, awaye
          Let's go, Sayo, let's go
SAYO   eala
          Lord! [invoking the Muslim Allah]

Note that Sayo's opening line gives the chorus its clue as to what it should respond with.

His playing of the kututeng in this song and others is resolute and firm but lacks the intricacy of movement and sound that characterizes some other musicians' playing. It is as if his kututeng accompanies his voice rather than balances it in weight, as it does for some other players. His musical strength is in his voice.

Type II Songs

In the type II song text pattern, the chorus repeats exactly what Sayo sings. In this particular recording session, he goes on from type I to type II, although this is not always the case. He starts with the kututeng alone, then sings as well, and then continues to play as the chorus voices its part.

SAYO   kamalakitande kenterina be
          By creeping with someone's wife there everything
          will start [trouble begins]
CHORUS (the same)

SAYO   iyee mandiwo iyeeyee
        [He says these are just sounds, a way of greeting
        someone, but they appear to mean "yes, hello,
        yes, yes," stretched out in song]
CHORUS (the same)

Next he sings the first line with which he started this section, and
the chorus repeats it. This is followed by:

SAYO   kaniakiro kentiri nabe
        Through discussion with someone everything will start
        [referring to lovers]
CHORUS (the same)

Now he goes back to earlier phrases in this section. Then:

SAYO   eh kpetawa kentiri nabe
        To escort someone everything will start
        [referring to lovers]
CHORUS (the same)
SAYO   kama konoko kentiri nabe
        In waiting for someone everything will start
        [referring to lovers] .
CHORUS (the same)

Then he stops.

Both of these types of singing seem to require quick and sensitive vocal reactions on the part of the chorus, but the responders
seem to have no difficulty reacting that way.

Type III Songs

The type III song text has no chorus at all but is a recitative, a
style of singing common in Sierra Leone (van Oven 1981:30–31).
The musician sings a series of lines, each without accompaniment,
and follows the line by playing a phrase on his instrument. Sayo

considers this sort of recitative to be singing (*asonki*) and not talking (*hugbonkiya*). One line may be repeated a number of times, each followed by an instrumental phrase without voice, before the singer goes on to the next line. The contents of the lines are a melange referring, like the song texts I have already described, to lovers, to Sayo's burial, to his blindness, to greeting me and others present, and to birth, death, and the lack of children. Some lines are like proverbs or sayings on life's ways. The type III pattern, requiring no chorus, is, of course, an easy one for the instrumentalist to use when playing alone, but Sayo also sings it when a crowd is present. The listeners often clap as he sings and plays. Sayo is the only one of the three musicians I studied to employ recitative. His use of it may be related to his having been a storyteller, for at Bafodea storytellers characteristically play and sing while telling their tales.

This recitative style is a dialogue between Sayo and his instrument, which acts as the chorus. The audience remains relatively quiet. In the performance I have been describing, Sayo went next into this song pattern after performing in the type II style, but he does not always perform in the same sequence. He may sing type III songs after type I or even before it.

In this performance, before going into type III music, Sayo started with a little Tenkele music and then went to type II style, singing as he played, the chorus responding.

SAYO   iyaka yama fonfe kanu nadome fonfe
        If you abuse me [insult or mock me] it is all right,
        it is God who did it to me [made me blind]
CHORUS (the same)

From that point on, there were no vocal responders, only some clappers, as Sayo sang alone in type III style.

kalana me kande mbembe toneno, wora mbembo toneno, iyaka yama fonfe kanu nadome fonfe
I say thanks to Kande [a woman's name], what is worrying you?

My friend, what annoys you? If you abuse me, it is all right,
it is the Lord who did it to me

nantukuse kututeng kunanoma manki, iyaka yama fonfe kanu
nadone fonfe
When I die, Kututeng music will bury me [be played at his burial].
If you abuse me it is all right, it is the Lord who did it to me

yo, metalobeye kandabamatoni, ka sakateloko, ninakahyi,
kere ba ma yanka
Yes, I have had bad luck, Handa [man's name], don't give me
trouble, I have come to explain. So the way the world is.
Don't exaggerate what I am doing [don't make a point of it]

yankindi ka holeonandu yan sitani
I started learning [the kututeng] when I was in my mother's womb

toro bina bayunkwin hati kakayunko
Struggle, people, for giving birth, the child is not in your hands
[has died]

yoooo, ninono kahaydo
Yes, I'm surprised, so the world is

toro beni pauli bembe tite yame
Struggle, Paul [Hamidu], these people have spoiled me
[made me blind by witchcraft]

yankindi kaholeonanda yan sitani
I started playing when I was in my mother's womb

yiki ba kutanki, metiba naluwe
Corn you say is nice, but later you take out the husk and open it,
the town is bitter [a proverb comparing corn and a town. The corn
is nice looking with its cover, but once you take off the husk you

have no respect for it, you are ready to eat it—just as someone in
the town will appear to support you but will not]

nantukuse kututeng kunanoma namki
When I die, Kututeng music will bury me

suma, ntenka mamina
Simon, I have come to spend the night [to play for you tonight]

walibena, walibena, bendoko luye sayo na
Thank you, thank you, for listening to Sayo

kalananiba keni
Thanks to people who give birth

yiki ba kutanki, metiba naluwe
Corn you say it is nice, but later you take out the husk and open
it, town is bitter

ntenka namina suma, mande suma
I have come to spend the night with Simon, hello Simon

toro bini wiya
Struggle, you people

hamidu, ntenka manina
Hamidu [referring to Paul Hamidu by his Limba first name],
I've come to spend the night [to play for you]

hamidu, ntaloko kahaydo naye bekiyebe
Hamidu, if the world does not fit you, give way to the people who
give birth [if you don't have children, give way to those who do]

terehe hita moneba bana santa
It is nicer to start with hard times than to end with them

nantukuse kututeng kunanoma manki
When I die, Kututeng music will bury me

toro bene na done
Struggle, take load later [if you do not have a child and you die,
people will take responsibility for your burial]

alatono ndo niyindi kiyeye kohoaido alana tetuwe
Mother-in-law, I wanted to give birth but the Lord does not allow

Sayo has no children; his brothers have them. The last line, like
others referring to lack of children, suggests his own condition in
a society where, without children, one has little status no matter what one's other accomplishments are. It may also refer to his
acknowledged impotence. *Tono* (mother-in-law) is a general term
used to address the mother of a spouse, the mother of a spouse
of one's child, members of one's surname group (these are large
groupings at Bafodea), and any female whose name a man does
not know. The term is often employed in singing at Bafodea,
sometimes in its first meaning but frequently in the general sense
of "woman."

Now Sayo goes back to earlier lines, interspersing them with
an occasional new one such as

nthoro bena masala gbaleyum
Sorry, the Lord has appointed me a musician

Then he goes on to new material:

sayo, bembe konde malo
Sayo, let everybody explain his problem

He repeats this, then:

suma alapalena
Simon, the Lord has written your name [decided your fate]

yankalana masala alaplena
I say thanks, the Lord has written your name

sori, yan yuwende keyinda
Sori, I have never heard your name

Pa Sori Mansaray, a young elder who is listening and who was himself a musician in his youth, is the eldest son of Pa Salifu Mansaray, the "big man" of my neighborhood and a chiefdom leader in
Bafodea Town. The line suggests that Sayo has received no dash
from him.

netalo maduno masala maka nina
If the place you settle, Maka, does not fit you, the Lord has written
your name for that [the Lord has determined where you should
live, Maka, you should accept it]

yan yuwende kenda maka, nayi ba tieti benayi
I have heard your name, Maka, a man who cannot arrange
anything without spoiling it [an old friend of the musician,
Maka is present at the performance]

maka na batinonde
maka na basukon
maka wo kututeng na yamboka
Maka sets quarrels
Maka makes people fight
Maka, the Kututeng music will bury me

To these comments about Maka, others present respond with
laughter; Maka says nothing. He and Sayo used to play the wooden
nkali together for farm work. Maka has a reputation in this part
of town as a troublemaker. This is one of the rare occasions in
Kututeng singing when a particular person is criticized, which is
perhaps tolerable because the two men are friends.

Sayo sings, "Thanks to Sori," then, "Thanks to Maka." Now
Sori gives Sayo a dash of some coins and Sayo responds:

yanke ye kalina, sori
I'm going, thanks to Sori

He does not actually go; this is a way of saying thank you, implying that now that he has been paid—now that he has received a
response to his music—he can go. Sayo says he sings such a phrase
when he feels good. We have also seen him employ it at the beginning of the performance, so that the same phrase may have different meanings according to when in the performance it appears.

nethaiyo maduno kanu kute
When things go bad, the Lord will see

That is, if you have nothing with which to support yourself, the
Lord will take care of you. Here Sayo uses *kanu*, the traditional
Limba term for Lord or God, rather than *ala*, the Muslim one,
which he also employs at times. Both commonly are used in the
chiefdom. Sayo is neither a Muslim nor a Christian.

yambe konde gbalo
Let me explain my problem

bembe ni nanene
They have promised me [if someone promises to do
something for you and fails to do it]

bembe nina kota
They have tricked me

nina kahayi abanta
So the world is, you will have problems

He goes on for a few more minutes in this vein. Like other Kututeng players, he has no particular song with which to end his
performances.

   In my field notes I say of this recitative that "it is like a series of explosions, with his voice going down to quiet at the end of each line and the kututeng becoming quiet, then starting up with another line to another explosion when the voice raises in strength and frequency." I found that this musical form—a series of lines sung without a chorus, each followed by instrumental playing either alone or in an ensemble, sometimes one line very quickly following another, and the lines often unrelated in content—was sung at Bafodea only by persons considered to be the better singers. I regard it as a skilled form of song involving much musical freedom and the ability to develop new lines and to maintain an audience's interest as listeners when people normally prefer to be active responders and dancers. People in the chiefdom, however, do not seem to view recitative singing as special, even though musicians, other people, and I all tended to agree on who were the better singers. Bafodeans view it as simply another way of singing and claim that a good singer needs mainly to have a clear, strong voice.

The Qualities of Sayo's Singing

There is a pervasive quality of personal lament—a sorrowful feeling—in Sayo's singing, interspersed with greetings to people present, comments about lovers, and proverb-like remarks such as "ma duno kaninde masa tenanda ewa" (there is no place that you will stay alone without others; that is, anywhere you go, you will not occupy a house alone). It has a fatalistic and passive quality as well: "It is the Lord's way," "The Lord has written it," "Witches have done these things." This quality contrasts with that of Sayo's very active life and musicianship, the life of a busy trader and performer.[5]

Sayo is quite free to choose the type of singing pattern and the particular words that he wishes, intermixing different topics at will. Like much of Bafodea music, his is not a rigidly constructed

5. Nketia (1973:96) describes a solo musician in Ghana, the basis of whose songs "was often some painful experience or something he felt strongly about."

musical genre. It is not strongly hedged in with rules about what should be performed at a certain time or how the music should be played. Sponsors of a major rite can often choose a variety of types of ensembles, and the chosen musicians are free to play the kind of music their ensemble represents pretty much as they wish. Taste and quality are paramount, rather than formality. There are some general requirements, however, in addition to conditions for treating the musicians. For certain rites, musicians are expected to play through the night (with rests). Second funeral music should always start with a type called Masande, no matter what instruments are employed; this announces the beginning of the rite. But there are no specifically designated musicians: sponsors may hire anyone they choose regardless of how well or poorly they play. Taste and financial ability, rather than formal position, dictate the choice. Even adolescents, of both sexes, often choose their own musicians for preinitiation dancing (although parents pay them).

This flexibility toward musicianship reflects that fact that Bafodea music is not directly tied to the ancestors, as is Shona music (Berliner 1978:chapter 8), or to other spirits, as occurs elsewhere in Africa. Such dissociation is particularly true of Kututeng because it is not specifically linked with major rites.

The recitative does not add up to a story or tale. Davenport (1984:44) suggests that "the Kututeng musician has not only the function of a musician creating rhythms and melodies to stimulate group dancing, singing and clapping, but of somewhat of a story teller as well, in the sense of an involved commentator who emotes feelings, expresses values and dilemmas concerning daily life situations." Of course, unlike Muctaru and Marehu, his fellow Kututeng musicians, Sayo was once a storyteller, which at Bafodea often involves nkali playing and singing as well as talking.

What comes out of Sayo's performances is not so much the contents of the songs as their sense of sadness and misfortune, of a lack of ability to control life or destiny. Yet the words do not create evident sorrow for the chorus, whose members appear to be happy as they sing, dance, and clap or, if Sayo is performing a recitative, listen, clap, and talk. The crowd seems less concerned with the words, which they know or quickly learn, than with the enjoyment of responding in song, clapping, dancing, and suggesting to Sayo during breaks their favorite lines to be sung. It is as if there is a kind of disconnection between the songs' words and those present at Sayo's performances. Through song, matters that are sad or disturbing or conflictual (but usually not political), which are otherwise private, can be publicly expressed, giving people as groups a chance to deal with the reality of their feelings under the appearance of happiness.

The importance of the event appears to lie in the activity rather than in the text: activity is all (Bourdieu (1977). Much of the activity is bodily—the playing of the musician, the singing of the instrumentalist and the chorus, the clapping and dancing. In Kututeng music, bodily experience is emphasized rather than complex verbal symbolism, a point Michael Jackson (1983) makes for the Kuranko, a people who live east of the Limba.

The repetition of lines, particularly in song types I and II, may itself produce a lack of interest in and concern with their content. As Gregory Bateson (1973:240) suggests, the better people know something, the less conscious they are of knowing it. The act of responding to Sayo's playing and singing is more germane to the chorus in some ways than are the contents of his lines. The "meaning" of the performance probably lies in the cognitive quality of the song texts more for me, in my search for clues to meaning, than it does for Bafodeans. For them, "meaning" lies in the act of doing, in the repetitive quality of the performance. Yet people do have favorite lines which they ask Sayo to perform.

All three types of song text patterns occur in other musical forms in Bafodea, so Kututeng fits well into the general musical tradition—it is not unique to it. The kind of response people make to this music as children is the same kind of response they will make when older to a variety of other musical forms with different instrumentation and song texts, although the songs' contents may be similar. Kututeng is good musical education and experience for children, albeit spontaneous and voluntary. It prepares the child to take part as a responder in ensemble performances when he or she is an adult. But Kututeng is not exclusively for children; some adults seem always to be involved.

The song texts are probably one unintended way of educating children to some of the unfortunate realities of adult life, which they will one day encounter. Sayo's songs stress adultery, witchcraft, troubles, and death. For children, who are not yet fully socialized and who may resent parental rules, some of the mood of the singing may relate to the songs' commentary on how adults frequently break the rules through adultery, witchcraft attacks, and so on. Children may feel vicarious enjoyment of rebellion against parents and others in charge of them: the songs are a sign that adults break rules which children are expected to follow—even though my impression is that children, at least in Bafodea Town, often are not well supervised by their busy parents and sometimes stay up late at night, long after their parents are asleep. For women, who usually make up the majority of the adults in the chorus, the songs indicate that their husbands and other men who have a role in controlling them are themselves not above breaking the rules.

Kututeng performances usually take place on the porch of someone's house. Other musical forms are also building-oriented. Generally an ensemble plays just outside the front of a house, sometimes that of the musicians' patron, where a large crowd can gather and dance. In ensemble work, the group often visits other homes, followed by a crowd (Ottenberg 1993). But once the Kututeng musician has attracted a following, he usually remains where he is, whether he is blind or not. The association of music with dwellings at Bafodea is a strong one, except for music pertaining to some secret society activities. Kututeng music is no exception.

Sayo is very much aware of whether he is carrying the chorus with him or not, particularly of whether people are responding in song and with clapping. At one point in a performance he sang:

walibena, walibena, bameyni bin kaholeho nandan masalana
kpeleyama
Thank you, thank you, people answer to me. In my mother's
womb the Lord wrote my name [decided my fate]

At another point he said to those present, "Why are the boys standing there not answering me?" I had thought he was getting a good response, but he was not satisfied.

Although there is no precise pattern in what type of song Sayo begins and ends his performances with or in what order he sings the song lines, his arrangements of them may depend upon his following. If a crowd has already formed, he is likely to begin, after playing some Tenkele, with type I or II music because it involves his listeners immediately in response, holding their interest. If there are few or no people about, he may begin with type III, the recitative, to attract listeners. Later he may switch to other types as people gather, and then perhaps resume type III when he feels he has a hold on his audience. Or he may simply play Tenkele music until he attracts a following.

In the first part of the session I have just described, people gathered quickly and Sayo followed this pattern of types: I, II, III, I, III, I, III, I, III, I. My impression that he performs type II less frequently than the others is consistent with the pattern in this particular performance. Type II music is perhaps less versatile and more constrictive a form because the chorus is bound to repeat his line immediately after he sings. His patterning of the three types makes for interesting contrasts. I can see what Nketia means (1974:139) when he writes that "the art of the *mbira* performer lies not only in the formation of chorded sequences and melodic patterns, but also in the appropriate use of vocal tones, melodic phrases or complete songs."

Sayo Classifies His Music

Toward the end of my stay at Bafodea, I asked Sayo to classify his music and singing as I was doing for the other two Kututeng musicians, Muctaru and Marehu. Of the three, Sayo seems least concerned with such matters. He says that most of his music is just Kututeng. Or he calls it *toro*, "struggle" or "hardship." By this he means music that centers on his blindness, his life, and his sorrows, and those of others. Of the three musicians' music, Sayo's is closest to his personal life. His are songs he makes up himself, he says, not anybody else's, although in fact he sometimes employs the words and melodies of Kunkuma and Poro musical ensembles, particularly in singing type I and II verses (Ottenberg 1993).

I press him to list other types of Kututeng music, and he plays what I later learn are two old and traditional Kututeng dance forms without singing—Warana and Tindotin. In addition, he can imitate Mankonkoba farm-clearing music on his kututeng; ordinarily he plays this type of music on the nkali with another musician. Although he plays the rhythm of Mankonkoba on his kututeng for me, the words are not the words he sings at the farm but his usual personalized lines. For example, with chorus repeating:

eetoro bambi toya
masala makama toya
oo masala nindema toya
ee bamakoreke toya
bamakun koreke toya
bamakun koreke toya

Eh, much trouble, true
The Lord has written my name, true
Oh, the Lord has done me bad, true
Yes, don't blame me, true
Don't keep blaming me, true
Don't keep blaming me, true

Thus he turns the Mankonkoba music into a recitative for me. Most of these lines are characterized by an initial and final word set off from the main phrase, a pattern sometimes seen in his other recitative vocalizations.

Magic and Religion

Sayo employs no magical charms, medicines, or sacrifices to help him sustain a performance or determine its quality, nor do any of the Kututeng players I know. Some instrumentalists and singers who are frequently hired to perform at major rites and who are thus in a more competitive musical market do so to ensure their popularity and success in performances. Sayo occasionally sacrifices for his general welfare, which includes his musicianship. Yet the need for a responsive chorus would seem particularly strong in a blind musician like Sayo, who otherwise cannot attract much interest in himself.

Although he employs no magic, so far as I know, some people believe Sayo has a "devil" (*wali*, a general term for spirit). Many Bafodeans believe that every exceptional musician has one that guides and helps him, but they are unsure about the specifics of its appearance and actions. They say, "Sayo yawu ewali" (Sayo has a devil). People with unusual skills or power at Bafodea are often thought to have the assistance of a wali. In a sense, this belief about Sayo is people's way of expressing recognition for his musical abilities. Others, however, seem to feel that he is exceptional as a musician because of his skill in playing a number of instruments in various types of ensembles, not only because of his kututeng playing. Neither of the other two Kututeng players I will discuss, Muctaru or Marehu, is believed to have wali, although Marehu's ability on the kututeng is much admired.

Sayo is unusual in that he rarely performs traditional Kututeng music, except occasionally Warana and Tindoten, but has created, using his instrument as his base, his own corpus of unique songs not taught to him by others. He and others call it Kututeng but recognize that it is his own creation and not traditional music. In addition, he plays some Kunkuma and Poro ensemble music on the kututeng, as Muctaru and Marehu also do.

Sayo in 1988

On my return to Bafodea for a brief visit in 1988, I found Sayo — always seemingly well informed about major rituals and events — playing at the chiefdom courthouse in Bafodea Town, where the Honorable P. H. Kamara, then acting federal Minister of Land

and Natural Resources, a Bafodea man, had come with important chiefs to settle a land dispute between Bafodea and the neighboring Limba chiefdom of Wara Wara Yagala. Other musicians were at the courthouse and also performed there before the discussion began and during breaks in it. The appearance of volunteer musicians, including Kututeng players, is usual when important visitors arrive in Bafodea.

In the evening of that day, another Kututeng player, Marehu Mansaray, with whom I had worked in 1978–80, came to greet me and play for me. He brought out a variety of musical forms with only a little quiet singing, which I recorded. Into this scene came Sayo, rather taking over, and I recorded him as well. As my notes indicate: "Marehu was very polite about Sayo doing so; to my apologies Marehu says they are both musicians playing the same instrument, they are both in the same trade, so it is all right." I am reminded that Sayo did this once with the third Kututeng player I worked with, Muctaru Mansaray, during my earlier research trip. There is a certain assertiveness about Sayo, an aggressive need that reflects a strong desire to be recognized, whereas Marehu is a quiet person and musician.

On this return trip I conducted a second funeral rite (*huboga*) for the grand elder Pa Salifu Mansaray, my "father" and wise guide at Bafodea, in whose compound I had lived during my earlier research. For this elaborate and costly ceremony I hired three ensembles as well as Sayo and Marehu to greet and play for the numerous guests. At first Sayo and Marehu performed individually, and then in the evening I found Marehu playing the kunkuma — the large box lamellaphone — and Sayo the kututeng, with another Limba striking the iron U-bar, kongole, in a Kunkuma music ensemble. Later that night, Sayo and the U-bar musician joined a different musical ensemble, Poro, which included a wooden nkali and a large huban drum. By this time, Marehu had left. This musical flexibility is common at Bafodea. On all these occasions Sayo's playing seemed the same as it had during my research some eight years earlier, with its strong vocal line, his enthusiasm, and his desire for attention.

Some two years later I learned that Sayo was dead, not yet an old man. His life was sometimes troubled, but he gave and received joy through his music. Despite his blindness, he led an active life as a musician and a trader.

4 Muctaru Mansaray

yeeyiyee kadi yandama yankutende kulonkpong
yeeyiyeeye sahinaba tatina kutakiki waniya!
Yes, yes, Kadi, here am I, I've got a love whom I love best,
Yes, yes, like my soap, wake up, it is daytime!

I MET MUCTARU MANSARAY OF BAFODEA TOWN ONE NIGHT
in October 1978, shortly after I had arrived, when he strolled to
my home carrying an eleven-tongue kututeng much like Sayo Kamara's in appearance, with the loose metal pieces attached to the
buzzer missing (figs. 13, 14, 15). He carried with him his baptismal
certificate from Kenema, deep in the country of the Mende people
in eastern Sierra Leone. There he had trained in crafts at the Centre for the Adult Blind for some twelve months beginning in March
1976, learning to make baskets. I never asked him why he brought
the certificate to me, but I presume it was because it showed he
had some training in the Western way, and thus I would understand him.

After greetings, he sat down on a chair on my porch (fig. 16)
and played. I was surprised at how quickly a gathering of children appeared and sang with him. Later I discovered that this was
almost always so with Muctaru: he is a favorite of the children
of the town, an African Pied Piper, almost always able to attract
the young—more so than Sayo Kamara or Marehu Mansaray, his
fellow kututeng musicians. But that night Sayo came too, inter-

rupting Muctaru's playing. We were unable to talk until a few days later, when we met at his home, down the street a little from my place, where he was living with a brother and the brother's wives.

Throughout our conversation, Muctaru seemed depressed, lonely, and uncertain. I ended up feeling very sad, as if my anthropology background somehow had little to do with reality. He showed me a hand cultivator, a hoe, and a digging fork, all new and of European manufacture, which he had been given at the blind center but had never used. The tools were somehow connected with me, a "European" in his town, and certainly not with Limba farm tools. But he had no one to help him grow vegetables, he said, having no wife, and women do not like to marry blind men—other women laugh at one who joins with a sightless man. Since he could not farm, he could not support a wife.

Muctaru's Life

Farming was how his eye trouble began, Muctaru says: a stick got into his right eye. He came home and slept and tears flowed from it, but it did not improve. He thought that perhaps the trouble was caused by wosi, spiders in the body which you cannot see. He was feeling cold in that eye. Although Muctaru was a Christian, his people told him to go to a diviner, who informed him, yes, the problem was due to wosi. He was annoyed that he could not see the connection between this diagnosis and the injury. "Pa" Decker, the American Wesleyan missionary living at Bafodea Town at the time, advised him that he could not be cured at Bafodea; he would have to go to Makeni, a city some one hundred miles to the south, but he did not go—no one took him to the doctor there. He was able to see out of the other eye well in the morning but not later in the day. So the trouble had spread.

A medicine man told him of a substance to put on his eyes, face, and head, a medicine that burns the body to kill the spiders. He tried this and it burned him, disfiguring his face and head somewhat, but it did not kill the spiders. He says he still has wosi: sometimes he can feel them crawling inside of him. Then his eyes

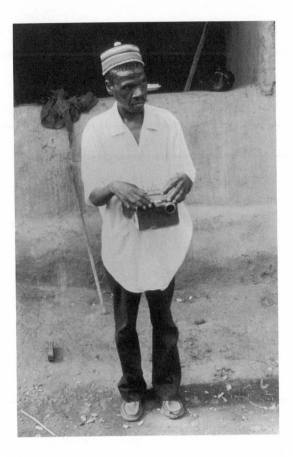

Figure 13. Muctaru Mansaray and his kututeng *in Bafodea Town.*

Figure 14. Mucturu Mansaray and his kututeng, *showing his finger positions.*

Figure 15. Muctaru Mansaray's eleven-tongue kututeng.

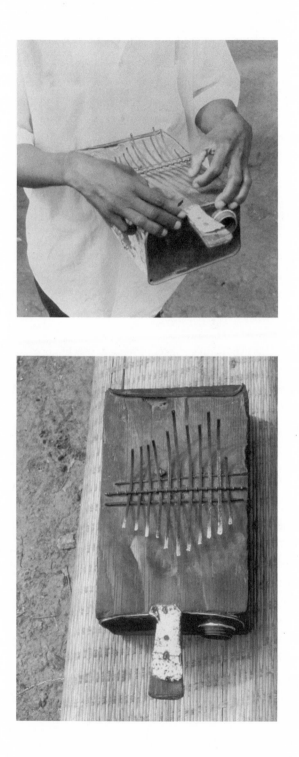

got worse and he went blind. "Yes, the spiders are still there," he informs me. At times his whole body is warm, at times cold. At other times it is as if ants are biting him; he is scratchy. "Where do the spiders come from?" I ask. As a Christian he says he does not believe in witchcraft. It is just a sickness he caught. He went to church in Bafodea Town before he went blind; he was baptized while at Kenema, in the Wesleyan church there, a very big building. He goes to church almost every Sunday in Bafodea Town, he says.

I marvel that he is willing to be so frank about his health at our first discussion, but he is obviously deeply troubled by his blindness.

At the time he went blind, a woman was living with him, but after some time she went away and later died. She had a daughter by a previous marriage, but no children with Muctaru. After the woman's death, a brother of the child's father took her away to live with him.

When his eye trouble started, Muctaru was living in his present room in his father's house. His younger brother Moci, who has two wives, occupies most of the building and feeds him, but only once a day when the wives return from the farms in the evening. He is hungry a lot of the time, he says, and I sense that there is some tension between him and his brother's family. One meal a day is not unusual in the chiefdom, however, especially for poor people, and even for others just before the year's rice harvest. But perhaps to a blind person food becomes more important, or perhaps the amounts Muctaru receives are small. I was eating three meals a day, which made me clearly a man of wealth by Bafodea standards. Muctaru's statements about hunger made me anxious, although I did not respond to them.

Muctaru says he did nothing for a while after becoming blind. He just sat. He had not been a weaver, although he had made sleeping mats, as many men do, some for themselves and perhaps a few to sell. A few years later a Mr. Kamara came to the chiefdom and told people about the school for the blind. He was going to all the chiefdoms in the area to recruit students, but Muctaru said some people were afraid to go, even though they were chosen, and did not leave home. He went, receiving seven Leones for the effort. At Kenema he learned to make baskets. He has two European pliers he was given, one for twisting bamboo, the other for cutting, and a long metal rod, made at home, to use in weaving the fibers. He learned to make a number of styles including the "No. 5 Madiera Neat," which is circular, a traylike shopping basket, and a Platseka —"plastic," although it is not actually made of plastic—which is a long container with a narrow neck. He showed me an unfinished No. 5 and a well-made, completed shopping basket (figs. 17, 18).

Muctaru makes baskets only occasionally, for he is dependent on someone else's obtaining the materials and helping him prepare the basket frame. He sometimes gets a boy to help him, but he has no one on a regular basis. A younger brother did this for a while but now has stopped. Muctaru earns much less for his baskets at Bafodea Town than he does at Kenema—three Leones for a Platseka there, and at home about one Leone twenty cents, and for the No. 5 Madiera, two Leones at Kenema and perhaps eighty cents to a Leone at Bafodea. People in Bafodea Town do not like the shopping basket, he says, and do not purchase it; it is apparently not in a form they prefer. When he has made something, he places it on the porch of his house to sell. If he is hungry he sells it cheap. I am angry that no one seems to help him much with gardening or with basket work; this adds to my sadness about him. Yet somehow I am reluctant to become involved, except with his music.

At the Kenema center Muctaru also acquired skills on the kututeng, the wooden nkali idiophone, and a European-style rattle with a wood base, the *shekesheke* (a Krio term), which is played in church. He did not learn to play the flute or the skin drum there. Unlike Sayo, he now plays only the kututeng, generally without other musicians but very occasionally in a Kunkuma ensemble whose members play the nkali, the metal U-bar (kongole), and the large three-tongue lamellaphone (kunkuma) (fig. 19). The kunkuma and the kongole are not played alone at Bafodea, although van Oven (1981:side 1, item 12 [discography]) records a Lokko musician at Makambi playing a solo kunkuma, there called the *kongoma*.

Another blind man from the chiefdom, Salifu, was at Kenema

*Figure 16. The house I lived in at Bafodea Town. Its porch was
too small to hold a good-sized crowd, which spilled out into the street.*

*Figure 17. Muctaru Mansaray's basket work: an unfinished
"No. 5 Madiera Neat" (left) and a shopping basket.*

*Figure 18. Muctaru Mansaray preparing bamboo fibers
from which to make baskets.*

with Muctaru; he lives at Kamagbemgbe, a farm village of Bafodea
Town, about ten miles from Muctaru's home. They both learned
to play the kututeng, as did Temne and Mende people and others
there, but Salifu was not good at it and does not play it now. No
one specifically taught the instrument at the blind center—its resi-
dents were there to learn basketry and gardening—but there was
a kututeng available and Muctaru learned a good deal of Kututeng
music from a Limba man from the Tonko area west of Bafodea.
Later a Lokko man came to Bafodea with a kututeng and Muctaru
bought it from him—the one he has now.

When Muctaru was young and had sight, before he was circumcised at adolescence, he had played the kututeng, and once
when he went with an uncle to Bo, in Mende country southeast of
Bafodea, he purchased one. He remembers playing it at the farms
as a boy when the lads were there for the ripening rice fields, driving away birds all day with slingshots, stones, and vine cords. Boys
bring along the instrument to amuse themselves at these times,
when there is little else to do but sit and talk and sing and chase
birds, and sometimes whittle figures out of wood. When Muctaru
grew up, he stopped playing, as is usual for Bafodea men, and he
had not played for a long time before he went to Kenema.

Does he play much now? I ask him. "Yes." When? Sometimes
he just plays in his room at night. Sometimes children in the neighborhood (who are not in short supply) come and sing and clap to
his playing. They are much about at night; they seem rarely to go
to bed as early as their hardworking parents. No one hires Muctaru
to play. If someone asks him to perform, he will do it, but they do
not ask him here, he tells me—only in Kenema, where he got paid
for this work. "Here they are not sorry for any blind person," he
comments. Since he does not farm or, usually, make baskets, he
sits most of the day at home or with friends in the neighborhood.

Although at Kenema he heard people play and sing Kututeng,
and although he brought some of that style home with him (a style
I have been unable to define clearly without published literature
to assist me), Muctaru sings in Limba at Bafodea, not in Mende,

the language of Kenema. He also plays and sings songs he later heard at home, but unlike Sayo and Marehu he rarely makes up new tunes and words for himself. He plays with Marehu, another blind kututeng player, he tells me. Muctaru admits that Marehu plays the instrument very well but says he cannot sing much. So he lets Marehu use his instrument, for Marehu lacks one of his own, and then Muctaru plays the kongole and sings with him. He says they do this for special occasions in town, but I do not think it happens frequently, because I have never heard them play together in this Kunkuma ensemble style. Marehu borrows Muctaru's kututeng and walks around town playing it, Muctaru adds. People come to hire Marehu, who plays the kongole and the kunkuma in Kunkuma ensembles, as well as the kututeng. But Muctaru complains that no one hires him, although he can play the kututeng while Marehu performs on the kunkuma. Now that Marehu has moved away to the other side of town, Muctaru says he sees little of him. Muctaru tells me that he cannot walk far: he is ashamed to do so, and he gets dizzy moving about. My observations confirm this; he rarely goes out of his neighborhood. In use of territory, in assertiveness, and in movement, Muctaru is Sayo's opposite, while Marehu falls in between.

At the end of this meeting I feel pity for Muctaru, who seems depressed, withdrawn, and defeated. My anthropological objectivity does not help. Perhaps this is why I offer to buy a basket from him which I do not need, which he will make for me. We agree on one Leone fifty cents for it, and I give him fifty cents for playing briefly the earlier night. He is pleased with this. He tells me that some blind people at the Kenema center sold their garden tools. He will keep his but has nobody to help him garden; he cannot do it alone. Could he get a small boy to help? He says he has no money to give children to work for him, as he is not making baskets now. Not long ago he made a shopping basket and showed it to the African pastor of his church—there is no missionary at Bafodea now—and said that this is what he could do, but the pastor did not buy it or assist him. And the trouble with the garden, he says, is that children steal the produce (which I have observed to be so). In the long run, I, too, failed to assist Muctaru directly, although I do have the shopping basket and I hired him to play a number of times. The basket, of a form he calls *blay* (a Krio term for basket), was finished about a year and a half after he promised to make it. A brother helped him get the raffia and native dye, and he made it in seven days. He made a second one of the same design. I paid him five Leones for one of them, forgetting I had agreed on a lower price. He was pleased. I believe he later sold the other one to the wife of the Bafodea medical dispenser, but for a smaller sum.

Muctaru's Performances

In September 1979 I had arranged to tape Sayo playing at my house one night but could not find him at Sakuta and asked Muctaru to come over instead. He brought along a nine-tongue kututeng he owned in addition to his eleven-tongue one. Pleased to be asked to come, he arrived with two women, Tene Mansaray, a full sibling, and Cuta Mansaray, of the same father as he but a different mother. They led the singing of a chorus of some forty boys and girls who soon appeared. Only occasionally have I seen Muctaru fail to attract a following of children. Yet once, the day before the start of a major Muslim second funeral rite in town, I observed that when he played on the porch of a house across the street from his own, no one paid attention. Perhaps the children were more interested in the many visitors who had come for the event.

Muctaru prefers to sit on a low stool rather than a chair; he rarely stands to play as Sayo sometimes does. Otherwise, his posture and the way he holds the instrument are much like Sayo's, though his body and arm movements are a bit more constrained. His voice is not as strong as Sayo's, but his playing seems more adept—he achieves a better balance of vocalization and instrumentation. He plays more on the instrument without singing than Sayo does. He does not employ recitative singing but uses the first two types of song texts I described for Sayo, both of which entail responders. He sings little of himself; although he is unhappy, his heart is not as open as Sayo's in his music. Like Sayo, Muctaru often repeats the same short song, sometimes for ten minutes or more.

Most of Muctaru's songs come from Kunkuma and Poro ensemble music carried over to the kututeng, and thus they are not traditional Kututeng forms. Their content has largely to do with lovers, often in adulterous situations. I am not surprised at this, since adultery is a common feature of Bafodea life, partly because girls are married during adolescence by arrangement of their families. Males marry at an older age, and when married they often seek new liaisons that may or may not turn into further marriages (Ottenberg 1988a, 1989b). Although Muctaru did not seem to have a woman when I was at Bafodea, he often sings of lovers. Of traditional Kututeng musical forms he can play three—Tindotin, Warana, and Kudingpon—whereas Sayo plays only the first two.

Muctaru begins, at this session, by playing the kututeng alone, starting with the Tenkele form, as is usual. Unlike Sayo or Marehu, he sometimes even begins and ends a song with it. He then sings:

mande, mande seki, mande eyuee
Hello, hello, Seki, hello, have you heard?

Seki is the late Dr. Siaka Stevens, former president of Sierra Leone and leader of the only political party in the country at the time of my research, the All People's Congress, or APC. This song was very popular at Bafodea, a strong Stevens and APC area, the president being partly of Limba background. People there told me that the day Dr. Stevens became president, the Bafodeans were very happy. Some boys went out and cut down a palm tree, the symbol of the Sierra Leone People's Party, the opposition party at that time, saying that the palm tree had been defeated by the sun (the APC symbol). They wrapped the tree in a white cloth and buried it in the graveyard. Muctaru thinks that this Kunkuma song was developed by the Limba of Sela, a western Limba chiefdom that has many migrants in all parts of the country. It is popular wherever Limbas are found.

But this is only the second line of the song, and later Muctaru

adds the first, with the chorus singing now, and he moves back
and forth between his two lines. Each time the group repeats what
he sings.

MUCTARU   papa seki, min ka, min ka kasela. Na papa seki min
           kayee kasela
           Papa Seki, let's go to Sela, Papa Seki, let's go to Sela
CHORUS   (the same)

In going over the tape of this song later, Muctaru, who is delighted to hear himself, says he has no particular song with which
to start a performance—he uses any one he likes—yet he has
chosen a popular one that will attract attention. Then, after numerous repeats while the crowd claps, as is usual during the singing, Muctaru plays the instrument for a while with clapping only.
Then he begins the song again, then plays to clapping, then the
song again, then playing without song. Now he is onto a new song,
one more local in content.

dumboloyee bebatunkoyee bakeyukutontaga wanda wanda tuketa
bebamakabe
Trouble [or danger] this is, it is very bad to tie the white band
while your husband is not dead. This is wonderful

When a woman's husband dies, she normally wears a white band
of mourning (*ntaga*) around her head at a certain time. But a married woman should not do this for a dead lover because they were
not married and her husband is alive. It would be amazing for
someone to do so. Note again that children are singing about quite
adult matters; they know full well about adults' affairs outside of
marriage. Then Muctaru goes to a second line of the same song.

MUCTARU   dumboloyee bebakabendo kulongbo yehita, igekuta
           bahino, namane babayehe
           Trouble, this is wonderful. The love is not yet all right,

they confess you [explain to your husband],
how will it be fine?
CHORUS   dumboliyee bebakabendo
Trouble, this is wonderful

My two field assistants, Paul Hamidu and Fatamata, discuss these lines, and one of them interprets the meaning for me. "Two persons are loving. Perhaps the lady has not given him any presents yet, or he her, and there is no sexual connection yet, but the lady goes and confesses to her husband. Now the man will not have a good mind to give her anything, or to talk fine to her. Maybe she has become frightened and told her husband right away." Again, following this song, Muctaru plays for a while as the crowd claps. Then he goes on to another song:

MUCTARU   yeeyiyee kadi yandama yankutende kulonkpong,
yeeyiyeeye sahinaba tatina kutakiki waniya!
Yes, yes, Kadi [a woman's name], here am I.
I've got a love whom I love best, yes, yes, like my
soap. Wake up, it is daytime!
CHORUS   tatina kutakiki waniya!
Wake up, it is daytime!

It is common in Kunkuma and Poro songs for the chorus to sing the end, or sometimes the beginning, of the lead line. In this lover's song, a man is talking about Kadi, his lover. Soap is prized at Bafodea. It cleans the body—it makes you feel good. If you go two or three days without washing, you feel unhappy. If you (a man) go two or three days without sex with a woman, you will feel unhappy.

After the usual repetitions, this song is followed by Muctaru's playing the kututeng alone, with the crowd clapping. Then:

MUCTARU   sandapalo sandapalo sandapalo yan kutubulu
sandapalo sandapalo sandapalo sandapalo yan
kamakeni nanke

I will not be afraid [repeated twice]. I am stout
[strong]. I will not be afraid [repeated three times],
I am going to Makeni

CHORUS   eyeee ewoho eyeyo mandengi kapaye
Yes, yes, yes, oh yes, yes, oh yes, our arrangement
did not last

The song is about a strong man who can travel far, to Makeni, the capital of the northern province. When you are not afraid you can travel far and be among other people without fear. The man laments that the love arrangement did not last.

All of these songs, except the first one concerning President Stevens, Muctaru learned at Bafodea. That one, he says, he acquired at Kenema; it is now popular at Bafodea. I do not believe he was the first to introduce it into the chiefdom—it probably came in through a Kunkuma ensemble.

I stop to change tapes, and Muctaru drinks some palm wine I have provided. He is smiling, and his beautiful white-toothed smile contrasts with his disfigured head. He is not at all depressed now, as he was at the earlier interview. There is lots of noise, talking—there are children playing on my porch and in front of the house, and people feel a sense of excitement. He goes on.

MUCTARU   yankuta beri ndo yungbo yankute biri nde
masalane wamba
I have burial young boys, I have burial,
God only has the light

CHORUS   woya yee yee woya yandiye kadiwoya
Sorry, yes, yes, sorry, pleased, Kadi, sorry.

The song refers to someone who has died, God only knows why. *Yungbo* is Krio for "young boys." Krio terms and sometimes whole phrases appear in Kututeng songs. Muctaru probably learned much of his Krio in Kenema. It has become a lingua franca for members of different ethnic groups in Sierra Leone, and most young and middle-aged people at Bafodea know something of this now nearly national tongue. Kadi is a popular woman's name, although no specific person seems to be meant here—a typical use of names in Kututeng singing. By its use it personalizes the song a little.

Next there is only playing and clapping, then the song again, then playing and clapping, then the song, then playing and clapping, a procedure Muctaru has employed before. In contrast, Sayo sings more continually and changes lines more frequently. Now Muctaru goes into the next song without a break.

MUCTARU   ilaiyela yon bonibe kotokanti mintene kamaka bie
          hurio ntehile
          Eh, my Lord, young boys, where will we sleep today?
          More visitors are coming, where will we sleep?
CHORUS   ayee eyun bo inehoye ayina yehohe
          Oh yes, young boys, please, young boys, please,
          my mother

When people go to a rite in a village, such as an initiation ceremony, there are often so many people that some do not have a place to sleep. I myself can attest to this. Muctaru sings, "Help me, my mother, to find a place to sleep." This is a song based very much on local experience.

He sings the first line, but the chorus does not respond properly. Some of them tell him they do not know their line and the song is too long. They ask him to stop it and he does. I note the tendency for the chorus to dislike long, complicated patterns, a preference also true for other Bafodea music, for designs made on wood and metal objects, and for other artistic areas (Ottenberg n.d.). I notice, too, that Muctaru is sensitive to the chorus's reactions to his playing. Now he tries another song, this time singing both his first line and the chorus's to let the latter know its part.

MUCTARU   yan madunuma yantimata ba baha yereme okawa
          How I'm looking. I don't like to love my
          companion's lady

CHORUS   yandiwo yandiwo yungbo timota ba baha yereme owa
Please, please, young boy, who doesn't like to love
his companion's wife

Muctaru explains, in going over this tape, that he does not like to
love a friend's wife. But he gives up on this song as well, because
again the chorus does not know it and cannot respond. Muctaru's
dependence on an effective response is considerable, since he does
not sing the recitative type of song. Sayo, on the other hand, can
go his own way. I am not certain why Muctaru is having trouble
with his chorus, but I surmise that it is because he is going beyond
what he usually sings, owing to my presence. The preceding two
songs may be from Kenema and may not be well known at Bafodea. Then:

MUCTARU   yereme wo kuta yan kapongbon dega mina
tugununde ebi konso bikonso bi done betamo mina
The wife I married at Kakpongkpon makes me
to quarrel with the Kakonso
people. The Kakonso people do not like me
CHORUS   ndokindo basahe kendundo
Very close, come back to your home

This is a popular song with many variants, referring in this case to
a man who marries at Kakpongkpon village, but the woman has
a lover at Kakonso and the people there do not like the marriage.
They sing for her to come home. Both villages are in the chiefdom; again, this is a song that is locally based.

Muctaru then goes on to the song about Dr. Stevens again,
then plays his instrument to clapping, then sings that song again
with its chorus, then plays his instrument. Next he stops and begins a new song:

MUCTARU   iyeeyee yan kandikpe koto mayagowo
awaye kanu awaye na yan ke

Oh yes, I did not know earlier, my beloved, O God,
O my mother

CHORUS   alikataya mingsing kudande, balohe sama dinyebe
Even if you wink your eyes at me, we shall see,
my goodness will not bring trouble to me

Fatamata interprets the meaning: "It is just about a man loving someone's wife. He is giving her things now and then, more than her husband. But he [the husband] suspects and tries to flog her to make her name the man. The lover sings to her: 'Let us stop loving to satisfy the fool. He will know we are not loving again. If I wink at you you will know what I mean.' The happiness that the lover has brought to the lady will bring trouble on him if he continues to love her." All of the foregoing are Poro or Kunkuma songs; often they are played by both kinds of ensembles (Ottenberg 1993).

Muctaru, as if dissatisfied with the audience's response to his singing, now plays Warana music (Davenport 1984:66–76), which boys and some adults love to dance to. The wild and energetic Warana dance is not done to Kunkuma or Poro ensembles. An old Bafodea Kututeng form, it is played only on the kututeng or the flute. My neighbor and friend, Suma Mannio Mansaray, a middle-aged man who is very skillful with his hands in many crafts, does the dance well. He twirls his body and stamps strongly with one foot, with body erect or swaying sideways or backward a bit, arms swinging loosely. Then he moves back and forth, stamping again, then twirls and stamps. Women dance the Warana too, though not as vigorously as men. The dancers are not in line but twirl individually, taking up lots of space. This night, at Suma's suggestion, they move off the porch to the earthen street in front my house, where there is more room, but they soon come back, preferring to be near the musician. Muctaru plays with strong beats, shaking his kututeng well to make the pebbles sound and doing variations on the tongues. He obviously hears the dancing and is stimulated by it. Then he stops for wine, which he is sharing with the other adults; the stimulation of drink adds to the excitement. All three of the

Kututeng musicians in this study perform Warana, a popular form at Bafodea and the only traditional Kututeng form they all play.

Now Muctaru goes into a Kunkuma song, but again the chorus does not respond. Everyone wants to dance Warana!

ooh wundewo dundun dine yande
Oh, my old friend, here am I

Then another Kunkuma song, to which he gets some response:

MUCTARU   yeyee wundema beya aye nande kahoreunde
           Oh yes, my sister, I will follow her where she is going
           to sleep
CHORUS   (the same)

Fatamata again interprets: "Two people are loving. The young man is talking to his sister, telling her he will follow his lover to where she is going to sleep." Then another song:

MUCTARU   eh wundewo dundo dinaya, kparakpara kokamkpara
           nabem koredama biyan binayan
           Oh, my old friend, here am I, the jealous women,
           if they kill me my people will take action on them
CHORUS   (the same)

Fatamata and Muctaru tell me that this is about a man married to a lot of women who are each jealous of his relationship with the others. He sings that if they kill him, his own parents or family will punish them. This is a well-known Kunkuma song. As he plays this, an elderly woman who has joined the crowd dances in front of him in the shuffling step of the Poro or Kunkuma dance, holding her body high. Then another woman excitedly dances on the porch. Now Muctaru sings the song about the man and his sister, but the crowd does not answer him and he complains about this. He moves his seat to the edge of the porch and plays Warana and the boys dance; dancing has overcome singing. Muctaru and other adults of both sexes continue to drink. I have provided three gourds of palm wine, a plentiful supply.

A little before 11:00 P.M., Muctaru asks how we are doing and I suggest that it is time to stop. I quietly pay him four Leones and thank him briefly, and he is very happy. I do not do this in the usual Bafodea manner, which is in public with a speech, often indicating the sum presented. I am shy about speaking publicly here, despite being a teacher at home. Perhaps I am also reluctant to reveal publicly what I have paid him for his Kututeng work because the sum is large by Bafodea standards. It has been a successful evening for him, even if the chorus did not always respond.

In a sense this was a contrived performance, arranged for me, but I believe from my other contacts with Muctaru that it shows his skills and capabilities well. Under more usual circumstances there would be no patron and little pay, only some coins from people following him. There would be little or no wine unless friends provided some. But there probably would be much the same Warana dancing and much the same crowd of children and adults, except perhaps fewer, if any, of Muctaru's relatives. Some of the adults were, I suspect, attracted by the palm wine as well as by the performance—there were some fifteen by the end of the evening. Probably, then, there would be somewhat less excitement. The evening was also contrived in that the two microphones for the tape machine took up space on the porch, and people were conscious of the equipment and my presence. Perhaps these factors had a dampening effect, although by this time I was well known at Bafodea as one who loved Limba music and dance and was not of a missionary mind.

When Muctaru, like others I have taped, played one piece for a very long time, I cut him off to start another. This prevented me from getting the natural ending of some pieces but allowed me to save my limited supply of tape and batteries to record a wider range of his music (there was no electricity in or near Bafodea). At the same time, Muctaru may have put more effort than usual into his playing and singing, knowing that I was there and that he was being recorded. These artificial conditions were recreated when I had Muctaru, Sayo, and Marehu each perform at a separate session, playing every kind of music they knew, one style after the other (Davenport 1984:191). The performance will inevitably be altered when there is an outside observer. Nevertheless, I believe the quality of this performance exemplifies many of Muctaru's talents. It certainly threw a different light on Muctaru in comparison with his depressed state at our earlier meeting. With music, Muctaru comes alive!

Although this was not the best performance event for Muctaru, since the chorus did not respond well, his playing, like Sayo's and Marehu's, normally gets a good chorus response in voice and clapping and sometimes in dancing as well. When each song is repeated for perhaps ten to fifteen minutes, often with little variation on the instrument, the meaning of the words apparently becomes quite secondary (Blacking 1967:30–31), if the audience bothers to understand them at all. What becomes important is action, particularly bodily action — the singing, clapping, and dancing and the movements of the instrumentalist — bodily behavior which Jackson (1983) considers primary over vocalization. Blacking (1977, 1987) believes that music is basically an experience of the body.

During the performance, the audience appears to feel a mild state of dissociation from the everyday. This state is probably stimulated not only by the repetition of a song with only minor variations (even consecutive songs may be fairly similar) and by the participants' common musical experience but also by the fact that two senses of time are being experienced at once — what Alfred Schutz (1951:89–90) calls inner and outer time. The time of everyday life exists as an outer frame. Inner time, which may seem faster or slower than outer time, is created by the music. Everyone involved — listeners, participants, and musicians — experiences both outer and inner time simultaneously. Blacking calls these two elements actual and virtual time. He writes that "daily experience takes place in a world of *actual time.* The essential quality of music is its power to create another world of *virtual time*" (Blacking 1973:37, italics his). He further states (Blacking 1971a:38): "The virtual time of music may help people to experience greater intensity of living."

Schutz (1951:88–89) also suggests that anyone involved in the performance "is led to refer what he actually hears to what he anticipates will follow and also to what he has just been hearing and what he has heard ever since the piece of music began. The hearer, therefore, listens to the ongoing flow of music, so to speak, not only in the direction from the first to the last but simultaneously in the reverse direction back to the first one." Schutz is apparently writing about Western music, with its considerable changes and development as it is performed. Does his observation apply to Bafodea, where there is considerable repetition over time of short song phrases and instrumental music? In Bafodea there indeed seems to be a condensation of the past music, that of the present, and that of the future—a movement from the past to the future and the reverse at the same time—that would add to a sense of dissociation from outer time and events, carrying those involved more into inner time.

Under these conditions, it would seem that individual identity is partly merged with that of the group (Blacking 1967:197–98). The merging is probably reinforced by shared somatic states (Blacking 1977:9-10). For the chorus there is common bodily experience in singing and clapping, sometimes in shuffling of the feet, and occasionally in dancing, which adds to the sense of dissociation from actual time. The blind musician cannot see this action but senses it through the sounds of the singing, clapping, and foot movements.

It is curious that the Kututeng song texts often have to do with discord—with witchcraft, troubles arising out of illness and adultery, and so on. Perhaps discord becomes less important because the meaning of the texts becomes submerged through repetition, the double sense of time, and the feeling of group identity. Yet the texts do help teach the young something about the adult world and its foibles, in which they themselves may become involved in the years ahead. For adults, the song texts reinforce the reality of their world.

If this analysis is correct, it suggests that, as an anthropologist, I am perhaps placing too much weight on the analysis of texts in

this book—on information I can get with a tape recorder and assistance in translation—and not enough on the emotions and feelings generated by the music, more difficult data to collect. I have
always seen texts as important clues to the understanding of a culture's workings. But I suggest that although to the young (and to
the anthropologist) the texts are useful in learning the culture (and
explaining it to the reader), what may be more important to the
participants in a performance is the activity associated with the
music, rather than the songs' textual meaning. The cultural importance of activity might be said to resolve the apparent contradiction in much of Kututeng music between the unhappy material of
the texts and the considerable joy in the performance.

Muctaru, who generally plays and sings not old, traditional
Kututeng pieces but Kunkuma and Poro ensemble music trans-
posed to Kututeng, is an agent spreading popular culture in Sierra
Leone. Some of his music he acquired at Bafodea and some at
Kenema; these two ensemble forms are widespread in the country and have been moving northward from non-Limba territory to
the south. His songs not only praise the president, refer to lovers,
and comment on death and burial but also remark on manly at-
tributes, traditional rites, friendship, jealously among wives—in
short, everyday experiences common to many adults in Bafodea.
They are reflections and commentaries on ordinary life.

In the Kunkuma and Poro styles, and in much of his other
music, Muctaru employs a fingering technique in which he plays
with two thumbs at once, whereas Sayo and Marehu usually play
one tongue at a time. Muctaru's technique is possibly derived from
Mende country, where he learned to play (Davenport 1984:157–61),
and it moves his playing toward a chordal structure. His voice is
neither as strong nor as rough as Sayo's, and he relies more on the
presence of other people who respond. His playing and singing increase in intensity as he goes on—the rhythm strengthens, there is
a growing sense of beat. In contrast, Sayo often starts on a "high"
and stays there throughout much of his performance. As an adult,
Muctaru has been playing only a few years, for his blindness is recent. Sayo, in contrast, is an old hand at the kututeng, having been

blind since boyhood and having played pretty regularly since then. Perhaps this accounts for some differences in their instrumental work and the sources from which they draw their songs.

Muctaru's Musical Types

Shortly before I left Bafodea I invited Muctaru to come and play on my porch the different types of Kututeng music he knew, while I recorded him. From this performance it became clear that he had a larger and more explicit set of categories than did Sayo, most of which Muctaru claimed he learned from the Tonko Limba player who taught him at Kenema. Some items in Muctaru's repertoire are imitations of other musical forms associated with ensembles, while others are traditional Bafodea Kututeng types for kututeng or flute. His nine-part classification is as follows, in the order in which he gave it to me, without distinguishing ensemble music from traditional Kututeng music.

1. *Kukangtan.* This music for second funeral rites is performed by a female leader's song and dance ensemble, an old ensemble form at Bafodea. Men play the wooden nkali, and women strike small drums, samburi. Here Muctaru imitates the beat of the nkali, and children and adult men and women dance for him without song, two short steps forward with the right foot, than two with the left. This pattern is continually repeated with the body bent forward slightly and arms at the sides—a shuffling, individual dance. Men and women dance it the same way. A man who knows how will go up to the kututeng player, as several did during this taping session, and beat a rhythm with both hands on the side of the instrument as it is being played. Davenport (1984:98–101) indicates that the music is in a two-phase pattern. At a real Kukangtan performance, many songs are sung and there is more elaborate dancing, especially in the lively and vigorous movements of the female lead.

2. *Kunkuma.* This ensemble, already much mentioned, has one characteristic beat. All three instruments—the three-tongue kunkuma lamellaphone, the iron U-bar (kongole), and the wooden

nkali—are played in a set pattern (fig. 19) (Davenport 1984:101–105; Ottenberg 1993). Sometimes the kututeng is also present. Muctaru plays Kunkuma much of the time on his kututeng; it is his predominant musical form, and we have already seen some examples. Its beat and style of dancing are similar to those of Poro music, but one of the instruments differs: the circular drum (huban) of the Poro ensemble is replaced by the kunkuma. Muctaru identifies some of the songs he sings and plays as primarily Kunkuma, others as Poro—though to confound the matter, the latter are also played by Kunkuma ensembles. For both ensembles the dancing is similar, the dancers moving slowly counterclockwise in a circle, as they do in much of Bafodea dancing. In Kunkuma, the musicians often are within the dancing circle. The dance steps are as I described them for Kukangtan except that the dancers move behind one another in a circle. Occasionally people come to the center to dance more vigorously.

Interestingly, the Kunkuma songs that Muctaru sings as examples of this music differ in content from ones he had performed earlier: during this taping session, many of them concern drink. Perhaps there was a hint of his needs in the words of these songs!

MUCTARU   bemang koraye woyi yala yando ba mampama
           bemang kora
           They will kill me for that, O God, for the wine,
           they will kill me
CHORUS   o yawaye bena koraye o yawaye
           Oh, lets go, they will kill me for that, oh, let's go

This is a song of palm wine tappers, a profession for which the Limba are famous. Muctaru is saying that when a man is tapping wine, people will go to him and try to get some for free. If he does not give it to them, they will want to kill him (but are not actually likely to do so).

MUCTARU   yunkan mylo bitiye
           Give me *omole* [local gin] to drink

Figure 19. A Kunkuma ensemble playing the large kunkuma *lamellaphone (left), the wooden* nkali *idiophone (right), and the metal U-bar* kongole *(center).*

CHORUS   (the same)
MUCTARU   enebiyue bisela papa wabatiye mylo inkunkuma
You have heard Sela [a Limba chiefdom], father, let
someone not drink omole while playing Kunkuma
CHORUS   (the same)

Later:

MUCTARU   yandiye wabatiye mylo inkunkuma
Please, let someone not drink while playing Kunkuma
CHORUS   o yandiyandiye
Oh please, please

Later:

MUCTARU   compin boy kupanti enintiye
My friend [in Krio], buy a bottle, let's drink
CHORUS   o yandiyandiye papayo wabatiye mylo inkunkuna
Oh please, please, father, let someone not drink omole
while playing Kunkuma
[*papayo* is from the English "papa"]

These songs express both delight in drinking at musical events
and fear that unsatisfactory musical performance, fighting, and too
much palaver may result if there is a lot of drinking, although such
disturbances happen only occasionally at Bafodea. When they do,
the sponsor of the music event can make a case against the dis-
turbers in court, or the elders may do so. A sponsor may, in greeting or talking to the musicians and the crowd in front of his house,
remind people that if they have had enough to drink they should
go home and not interrupt others.

3. *Warana.* I have already described this form of Kututeng for
dancing without song.

4. *Tindotin.* You can dance to this traditional Kututeng music,
says Muctaru. It is played on either the flute or the kututeng; there

is no singing. A number of people, usually boys or young men, dance in a small circle with steps much like those in Kunkuma dancing. Suddenly one of them turns his head toward the outside, making a distorted or ugly face and holding it. If you laugh at this, Muctaru adds, the dancers "flog" you, that is, whip or hit you. This practice seems to have derived from children's play, though adults at Bafodea also flog each other in Tindotin performances. Like Sayo's Tindotin music, Muctaru's has a five-beat pattern, with variations, and employs a two-phase structure, but at times he adds another beat (Davenport 1984:78).

5. *Kudingpon.* This is another dance, done by both boys and girls, generally with only a few songs, the musician and dancers singing together.

MUCTARU AND CHORUS   kendende kuloiloi
                                     Monkeys and their tails

Kudingpon refers to tails. This line is repeated over and over as the children dance in a circle, holding onto the belt or clothing of the person in front of them, taking exaggeratedly large forward steps but moving very slowly. Girls may dance Kudingpon around a settlement without a musician, singing as they move in single file. According to Davenport (1984:80–82), this is a four-beat repeated pattern with a syncopated fourth beat. Sometimes the words differ:

MUCTARU AND CHORUS   kuloiloi kenden tanken
                                       Tail monkeys finish

This has been interpreted for me as meaning that when the monkeys (with their tails) enter the farm, if there is any corn they will finish it.

6. *Kuberiberi.* This word is the name of a small, smooth-skinned lizard about one and a half inches long. There is one song, sung by the musicians and sometimes by the dancers at the same time.

yeeye koda bondiwo yelele madongama beteng hite helele
Yes, Koda Bondi [a man's name], to leave in a secret way,
yes, young men are happy to leave in a secret way

When this Kututeng music is playing, Muctaru says, young people will be happy, for boys will have a chance to see their girl friends and will quietly take them away. All dancers face the musicians, but not in a line. The dancers step forward with one foot and then step back in place; then they do the same with the other foot. This continues, the dancers imitating lizards, with arms loose at the sides and bodies bent forward a little. Sometimes this music and dance is called *kpunkimadada,* the term for a larger lizard that moves its head up and down a great deal. Davenport (1984:82–84) believes that the instrumental pattern is similar to that of the Kunkuma ensemble, although the vocal pattern differs somewhat. Our third musician, Marehu, who mostly plays traditional Kututeng, does not play Kuberiberi. This raises the possibility that this musical form is not an old and traditional kind of Kututeng, as Muctaru and some others think, or that an old form of Bafodea dance and song has been wedded to a newer musical form, Kunkuma.

Note that these last two forms, Kudingpon and Kuberiberi, are associated with and imitate animals. Many Bafodea tales and stories and some children's games also have animal referents.

7. *Gbondokali.* Muctaru imitates the beat of the long drum (kusung) and the iron bivalve kukenken idiophone of the famous musician Kaliwa (a Limba from Kasonko chiefdom, south of Bafodea), who was recently at Bafodea Town for the boys' preinitiation dance, Gbondokali. This music is actually played by a variety of ensembles composed of various instruments, often the two just named and the wooden nkali. As Muctaru plays, the boys on the porch try to imitate the cartwheeling and twirling of this dance, but there is no room to do so. Davenport (1984:110–13) analyzes Muctaru's Gbondokali playing as a repeated eight-beat pattern. During the ensemble performances there is singing, mostly by females, but none occurred here.

8. *Poro.* These are songs which Muctaru says can also be used

by Kunkuma ensembles, and the dance is the same. The ensemble generally includes a large circular drum (huban), the metal U-bar, and the nkali (figs. 20, 21). Muctaru here imitates the beat of the nkali wood gong in Poro ensembles. In this genre he sings for me the only specific burial song he says he knows that a Poro or Kunkuma ensemble plays at a second funeral; generally songs about lovers and troubles are sung:

MUCTARU   yan kpinki berinde mayaka yan kpinki barinde
          neyumbo
          I met a burial, my people, I met a burial,
          yes young boy
CHORUS   waya
          [a way of crying]
MUCTARU   masalana wamba
          The Lord has light
CHORUS   waya eyeee kadiwaya eyeee
          [a way of crying] yes, Kadiwaya [woman's name], yes

Note that although Muctaru is a Christian, he employs the Muslim term for God at Bafodea, *ala,* and elsewhere the Limba name Kanu. None of the three musicians I studied used the English word *God* in his songs, nor do the song texts refer to the Christian religion. The other Poro songs that Muctaru knows are like the Kunkuma ones I have already commented on. Davenport (1984:114) indicates that Muctaru plays the same instrumental pattern with both ensemble forms.

9. *Rainbow.* This modern music is played and sung during the Christmas and New Year holidays at Bafodea Town—the only place it exists in the chiefdom, so far as I know. The songs are in Krio or Limba or both. The instruments are a variable lot, often including the metal U-bar kongole, the three-tongue kunkuma lamellaphone, an iron single-valve or bivalve idiophone, several wooden nkali, one or more varieties of drums, and an oil pan from an automobile, which is struck with metal or a wooden stick. The kututeng does not seem usually to be included. Although its metal-

Figure 20. A Poro performance with nkali idiophone and dancers. The other two Poro instruments are not showing.

Figure 21. Two instruments from the Poro ensemble: the huban drum (left) and the nkali (right). The metal U-bar, kongole, is absent.

Figure 22. A Rainbow group with masked talabi *dancer*
at Christmastime.

lic quality might be appropriate, it would likely be drowned out by all the other instruments. Rainbow music is played by a large group of strolling musicians, perhaps difficult for a blind player to follow. Muctaru does not try. It is a performance often involving a masked figure or two (*talabi*), a group of female dancers and singers all dressed in similar cloth (*ashobi*), and a loose grouping of numerous males who also sing and dance (fig. 22; Cannizzo 1978, 1979).

As one might guess, this is an urban musical and performance form that apparently started in Freetown (Kreutzinger 1966:58, 71; Nunley 1987:200–202) and made its way to Bafodea Town in simplified form via Limba people who live or have lived in Freetown and other Sierra Leone cities. Rainbow at Bafodea is largely a young adults' group. Many of the performers have lived in Freetown and other Sierra Leone cities for periods of time; some are at home only for the holidays. Youth and modernity mingle in its performance. Davenport (1984:120–25) states that Muctaru's playing of Rainbow music on the kututeng is in a four-beat repeated rhythm with variations.

Muctaru did not mention Tenkele music, although he plays it, perhaps considering it a different type of music because it is a prelude or a form he sometimes uses to bracket other musical pieces. But like Warana, Tindotin, and Kudingpon, it probably represents an older stratum of Kututeng music at Bafodea. Gbondokali music is also old, but is not music characteristically played on the kututeng.

Muctaru's classification of Kututeng music is based primarily on the different configurations he plays on his instrument. As he lists the types for me, he is not particularly concerned, as this anthropologist is, with whether the music is drawn from ensemble music or is of an older, more traditional Kututeng form. He shows versatility in his imitation of musical ensembles and in his ability to play a number of dances. Despite his having played the kututeng seriously for only a few years (not counting his casual playing as a child), he plays with skill. If Muctaru, unlike Sayo, directly expresses little of his own heart in his music—and some Bafodeans think him the better musician for it—he does exhibit delight in variety, in playing for responding people, particularly children, in the amalgamation of traditions, in bringing new forms of music to Bafodea or at least representing them, and in the skillful blending of song and instrumental playing. He is modest about his own playing and singing, pleased by his following of children, but sore that he does not receive greater recognition for his skills among adults.

When I returned to Bafodea in 1988, hoping to hear Muctaru play again, I learned that he had died several years before, from what I could not determine. I have to conclude that it was probably the spiders, after all, in one way or another.

5 Marehu Mansaray

kulongkpon ka ma kika yan makan tete
Love is not like a cloth. [If so] I would get it on credit

MAREHU MANSARAY, BORN IN BAFODEA TOWN, IS A LITTLE older than Sayo and Muctaru (fig. 23). Although he and Muctaru have the same surname, they are not closely related—there are many Mansarays in Bafodea. When Marehu was young he was a farmer, as is typical of chiefdom men, but he was already a musician, playing the kututeng, the flute, the kunkuma, and the kongole. His eyes were already bothering him, and he went blind when he was about twenty-seven, around 1954, the year Bafodea Town moved to its present site. He claims it was God's way that he went blind; he does not speak of any other reason nor does he attribute it to witchcraft. Like Muctaru, he is a Christian, having been converted by Pastor Kargbo, a former town resident. He never discovered the cause of his blindness, although he consulted native doctors. He lived in Kabala, the Koinadugu district headquarters, thirty miles by road from Bafodea in those days. For three years he received treatment there from traditional healers and at the government hospital, but nothing helped. At times his eyes still irritate him.

He is of medium height, thin, and, unlike Sayo, generally neatly dressed in well-fitting clothes. He never married and lives in Bafodea Town with distant kin—what my field assistant Paul Hamidu

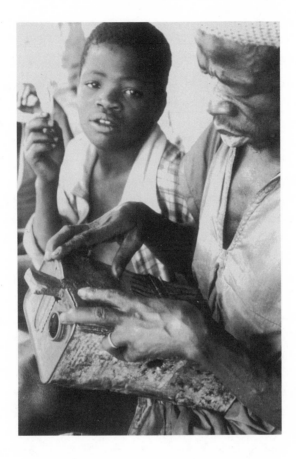

Figure 23. Marehu Mansaray playing Muctaru Mansaray's nine-tongue kututeng.

cynically calls "elastic" relatives. By this he means those who, when you are poor and in need, do not recognize any kin tie but who claim a connection when you are rich. Marehu shares with Muctaru and Sayo the problem of getting sufficient food at times. Once when I wanted to talk to him, he was too weak to walk to my house, so I went to his. He is not fed regularly, he claims. But he does some farm work, assisting his good friend Pa Modi Mansaray, a man not blind but also unmarried, the best and busiest weaver in town. His farm is located a few miles from Bafodea Town; Marehu helps Pa Modi clear the land and keeps him company. Like Sayo, Marehu is active. He walks around town a lot, though not to nearby villages, has a number of friends, and likes to visit and talk with people. Often he is on Pa Modi's porch when the weaver is working there. He does not seem depressed, as Muctaru was when I first talked to him, or sorrowful, like Sayo, but well balanced and adjusted, intelligent, and able to cope with his blindness.

Marehu began to learn the kututeng when he was about twelve years old. His relatives were pleased, he says, when he did this, though there were no musicians in the family. He taught himself to play but never learned to sing much and he does not do so now. He suggests to me that at the time of his childhood and earlier, there was much less singing and clapping by the responders in Kututeng music than there is at present. Kututeng then consisted mainly of instrumental music—frequently Warana—with the musician alone doing some singing and those present listening and dancing. Marehu sees himself as a player in this older Kututeng tradition.

I have heard him in the early morning, as he walks the streets of Bafodea Town alone, playing his instrument for the pleasure of it, sometimes singing softly to himself. I believe this practice is also an aspect of the older Kututeng tradition. It may be that much of the singing and clapping by the chorus associated with Kututeng music today came to Bafodea under the influence of the Kunkuma and Poro ensemble forms of music. Kunkuma ensembles, of course, sometimes include the kututeng in performance today. Kunkuma and Poro songs have been taken over for use in solo Kututeng music by some musicians, such as Muctaru and Sayo, as we have seen.

Marehu claims that before people moved from the old Bafodea Town to the new settlement in 1954, there were more kututeng players about than there are today. Others tell me that in those days some players were youths but others were men of middle age, mostly sighted. No one remembers the instrument's ever having been made of anything but commercial metal, although it is possible, if the kututeng is of some antiquity at Bafodea, that it was originally constructed of wood, with a wood resonator or perhaps just a wood sounding board. Yet all the like instruments that I know of in Sierra Leone are made from metal cans. The one-gallon tin is popular because it resonates so well and is so sturdy, Marehu tells me.

The older-style Kututeng is like flute music, Marehu says. He learned to play the side-blown flute (kutotiya) when he was young, shortly after learning the kututeng. He played the kutotiya late at night, just for himself, when other people slept, but also at other times for young boys who danced but did not sing or clap. He performed on it alone, not with other instrumentalists; he did not encourage others to play with him. The bamboo or wooden flute of the Limbas of Bafodea, but not that of the Fula people, is truly a solitary instrument. He stopped playing it a long time ago, Marehu says; it is not an instrument that adults usually employ.

The newer forms of Kututeng, which are related to ensemble music, appear to be played mainly in Bafodea Town. The older forms are played largely by Marehu there and by boys and young men in the Bafodea villages, which are generally more traditional in their music. The flute, too, is more of a village instrument. I once heard a man play the kututeng at Kamagbemgbe farm village. He played sitting down while boys and young men danced about individually and softly, in a gentle manner, with no singing. I have sometimes in the villages seen a man just walk about a settlement playing Kututeng music, with no singing or dancing. Occasionally boys in the initiation bush area will have one of these instruments; one plays it and the others dance to Warana, Kuberiberi, Kudingpon, and other traditional Kututeng forms. At a marriage ceremony in Siemamaya village, some ten boys went about, one of them on a flute and another on a kututeng. Later they joined an invited Poro ensemble. Sometimes men's farm-work groups will have a kututeng brought by one of the workers but played for amusement only when they are resting.

Like Sayo, Marehu is also an ensemble musician. He does not play music for farming but is a member of a Kunkuma group made up of friends from the town. He generally plays the kututeng with them, but he can also perform on the kongole and the kunkuma. I believe the kututeng is the oldest of these three instruments at Bafodea, but I could not obtain any stories of its origin, either secular or mystical, in contrast to the Shona mbira (Berliner 1978:45). When Marehu was still living at the old town site, the metal U-bar (kongole) came in with Poro music, which also employs the circular huban drum and the wooden nkali. Then, about 1949, American Wesleyan missionaries came to live in Bafodea Town, bringing a Tonko Limba carpenter, Pa Sama Kargbo. (The Tonko are the westernmost Limba people.) Not long after everyone moved to the new town, Pa Sama brought five apprentices from the Tonko area to help put up new buildings. Three of them came with Kunkuma instruments and music. A number of people at Bafodea, however, told me they did not think this music originated with the Tonko people but that it came from the Lokkos to the southwest. They believed that Kunkuma at Bafodea today used Lokko instruments and instrumentation combined with songs from the Poro ensemble, sung in Limba.

Be that as it may, the carpenter apprentices played only the U-bar and the kunkuma. Later they invited Marehu to play the kututeng with them, and that is how he learned Kunkuma music and eventually the other two instruments. In Tonko, people were playing Kunkuma both with and without the kututeng, Marehu says. These Tonko men taught a number of Bafodeans how to play Kunkuma and also made Kunkuma instruments for them.

The kunkuma is a simple instrument, with one basic beat in

performance and fingering for much of its music. The first Bafodean to learn it was Kadio Mansaray, who taught Samba Mansaray, with whom Marehu sometimes plays Kunkuma today. Kadio also taught Marehu, who later taught Pari Kamara, with whom Marehu also plays. All these men were living in Bafodea Town. Marehu had earlier learned to play the metal kongole, which also has but a single beat in Kunkuma and Poro music. It is easy to learn, though holding the instrument up while playing is tiring.

So, through a round of contacts, Marehu knows three instruments of the Kunkuma ensemble. After learning this kind of music, he played regularly in a Kunkuma group with two men who are now dead. At times they were called to play at second funerals. People at Bafodea say that Kunkuma music is not as popular now as it was before. Yet while I was in the chiefdom, Marehu's ensemble (which he himself does not lead) played as invited musicians for a number of second funeral rites in Bafodea Town and in one such rite in a neighboring village (although sponsored by a town man). Whether it is declining or not, some Bafodeans prefer Kunkuma to other musical forms because it is gentler and quieter.

Unlike the kututeng, which is found everywhere in the chiefdom, the kunkuma never spread to the northern areas of Bafodea —the old Kamuke chiefdom. (An exception is the village of Kambalia, one of the southernmost of these northern villages, not too far from Bafodea Town.) Kunkuma music today is found mainly in Bafodea Town and in the very southern village of Kadanso, where there are at least two ensembles, one started about 1969 and the other some years later. There, the Kunkuma musicians sometimes sing different songs from those heard at Bafodea Town but play the same instrumental music. They have been influenced by Kunkuma musicians from Limba chiefdoms to the south, especially Kasonko. Musicians from these southerly Limba areas are sometimes hired in the southern villages of Bafodea chiefdom to play at major rites, and some of their songs are known in Bafodea Town.

Marehu claims that most of the time, when his Kunkuma group appears in Bafodea Town it is not because they are invited but because they come out to some rite for the enjoyment of it and in hope of getting a little money. He has a kunkuma box—indeed, the only one in Bafodea Town—that one of Pa Sama's apprentice carpenters made for him, and he has a kongole prepared by a blacksmith. When I first interviewed him in November 1978, he had no kututeng but was using Muctaru's. His friend Salifu Mansaray, a carpenter and member of the same Kunkuma ensemble, was making him one and had made him others in the past. Marehu says that an earlier kututeng of his "spoiled"; he lent another one to a friend in a village and never got it back.

He prefers the kututeng to the kunkuma and the kongole because he can play it alone, whereas the other two instruments are never played singly. I share his preference, for of the three, the kututeng is the only melodic one; the others are primarily rhythm instruments. Marehu sees music as his "work" because he has no other, although he does not play often and gains little income from it. Although he knows Kunkuma music well, when he plays the kututeng alone he does not play Kunkuma songs on it, as Muctaru does, but the older Kututeng music, the more traditional forms. Marehu is a traditionalist on the kututeng, Muctaru has adapted to it a new form of playing associated with Kunkuma and Poro, and Sayo is an innovator with a unique style who also plays Kunkuma and Poro forms on the kututeng.

Marehu's Instrument and Playing

I talk to Marehu about one of the instruments he is using, Muctaru's nine-tongue kututeng. Marehu tunes it the way Muctaru and Sayo do, with each tongue roughly equidistant from those on either side. Marehu says he uses only one tuning for his repertoire. All five kututengs that I have examined closely at Bafodea look as if they are tuned roughly the same way, but Davenport (1984:171–81), using my tape recordings, indicates that there are minor tuning differences among them. Generally an odd number of tongues is preferred, but even-numbered instruments are also played. I have seen kututengs with thirteen, eleven, ten, nine, and eight tongues at Bafodea. Van Oven (1973–74:77) writes that nine is a favorite number of tongues in Sierra Leone; this number does not appear to have any mystical import at Bafodea.

Marehu has placed a pebble under each of the three longest tongues, in back of the rear bridge, to hold them firm. When he tunes a kututeng he begins from the two outside (higher frequency) tongues, one on either side of the keyboard, and then works his way toward the center tongue from both sides, plucking each tongue separately. Then, when he thinks all the tongues are set, he tries playing the instrument, adjusting the tongues by pushing them forward or pulling them backward as needed. He uses only his thumbs to play, like other kututeng players at Bafodea. When I ask whether he ever uses other fingers, he answers negatively and laughs, thinking this a funny question. Later I reflect that the anthropologist is always asking "funny" questions—it is impossible to avoid asking about what turns out to be the obvious. But one has to be certain, and Marehu does not object to such queries.

When he plays, Marehu presses down on a tongue and then slips his thumb off of it. The tongue swings up and down rapidly, making its sound. Many ethnomusicologists call this form of playing *plucking,* although Kauffman (1980:402) does not feel that it truly is. As Marehu plays, I realize that he fingers the outer-edge tongues on both sides more than the center ones and that the outer edges are where his thumbs are naturally placed as he holds the second, third, and fourth (or only the third and fourth) fingers of each hand over the far corners of the instrument (fig. 24). He does not like to put attachments on the buzzer, the wesewese, because he does not care for its sound. It is missing from the instrument he shows me, although he once had it on another kututeng. If he loses a tongue or it goes bad, a blacksmith makes him a new one. Davenport (1984:157) indicates that Marehu is the most versatile of the three Kututeng musicians, playing some forms of music with one thumb at a time and other forms with two. Sayo does largely the former, Muctaru the latter.

Marehu prefers to sit on a low stool with his instrument on the floor. In this position he can lift up the far edge of the metal resonator and slap it back to the floor to create sound when it hits. As

Figure 24. Marehu Mansaray playing Muctaru Mansaray's nine-tongue kututeng, *photographed from above.*

he does, the pebbles rattle inside, adding yet another sound to the playing. Like most Bafodea kututeng players, Marehu arches his wrists upward as he plays (Zemp 1971:38, plate 6).

The term for the kututeng's metal box is *kankiran,* a Fula term for box and a word employed by Bafodeans for any square or rectangular container. Its usage suggests that boxes of all kinds in the chiefdom are of foreign origin. I believe this to be the case, in contrast to baskets, which are generally circular and have local names. I do not think, however, that the kututeng came to Bafodea from the Fula, who do not play it, so far as I know. The problem is that Bafodeans do not know where it came from; they just say it is old.

Frederick H. W. Migeod (1927:83) thought it was introduced to Sierra Leone by West Africans who went to East Africa, where small lamellaphones occur, in the military during World War I. The Bafodea form appears to resemble forms of this instrument found today in southwestern Tanzania (Kubik 1980a:403). But George Montandon (1919:39–40, 101) sketched and described an instrument much like the Bafodea ones, with the wood projection but lacking the metal box and buzzer, which he collected in Sierra Leone in 1917 in Temne territory, south of Limba country. He thought the instrument belonged to a class he called "Type à Poignée de la Haute-Guinée." He also included in this category a similar instrument from Cameroon. Andre Schaeffner (1951:52) briefly mentions the instrument's presence among the Kissi of Guinea, not far from the eastern border of Sierra Leone. He describes a seven-tongue instrument on a curved piece of wooden bowl, played by boys and young men, which, however, is not widespread in Kissiland. If the Bafodea kututeng had a pre-metal box form, which is uncertain, it may have appeared something like one of these other types. Van Oven (1970:23–24, 25 [photo], 1973–74:82–83) writes that the kunkuma is generally called kongoma — its Temne name — in Sierra Leone and that it is widespread in the country (van Oven 1981:13–14, figs. 22–26; Lamm 1968:65–66, fig. 25).

I myself think it more likely that the kututeng in Sierra Leone came from southern Nigeria or Ghana, areas with which Freetown and its Creole society have had long-standing contacts, and that it spread from coastal Freetown to the interior of Sierra Leone. In these other countries, however, the instrument does not have the metal resonator but generally a half-gourd or wooden one. Some support for this origin hypothesis comes from Johann Büttikofer's (1890, vol. 2, p. 336) account of the instrument among the Kru of Liberia before the turn of this century. A coastal fishing people, the Kru have settlements in Freetown (one section of which is called Krutown) and elsewhere along Sierra Leone's coast. They fish as far north as Guinea and at least as far southeast as Ghana. The kututeng could have traveled to Sierra Leone with them.

Why the instrument is played in Sierra Leone in the reverse position from the way it is played in most other parts of Africa— that is, Sierra Leone musicians hold the playing part of the tongues away from the body—is unclear. Van Oven (1970:23) thinks this practice is followed only in Sierra Leone, but Zemp (1971:39, plates 5, 6) writes that among the Dan of Ivory Coast, it is the most common way of playing. His description of the method of playing the instrument and of its tongues and its tuning resembles that for Bafodea, although the resonator is a calabash (again suggesting a possible pre-metal box form for Bafodea). François Borel (1986:150–51) mentions a small lamellaphone from Danene in the same country; it has seven metal tongues on a decorated board tied to a half gourd, with a winged metal vibrator at the far end, and is played in the same manner as the Bafodea kututeng. I suspect that this reversed method of playing is sporadic in West Africa and more common than van Oven thinks, although I have no other record of it. Written accounts often do not say how the instrument is held and played, and it is not always possible to assess the matter simply by viewing an instrument or its photograph.

Is the position in which the kututeng is played in Sierra Leone and Ivory Coast a translation of body experience from some other musical instrument or work tool? Does it relate to some other common body motions in the cultures there? I do not know. I have sometimes conjectured that someone in one of these cultures found a kututeng-like instrument left behind by someone from a culture that played it the more common way, and the finder, not knowing the "correct" manner of holding it, began to play it in reverse, resetting the tongues in order to do so properly. This scenario might have involved East African troops in Freetown in World War I, or French African forces from elsewhere in Africa in Ivory Coast. But this is pure conjecture on my part; I lack any evidence for it. The matter remains a mystery.

No matter what the kututeng's history at Bafodea may be, it is considered a traditional instrument there today, even though some of the kututeng instruments played there were obtained outside the chiefdom: one of Sayo's from Kabala, and Muctaru's first one from Bo and a later one from a Lokko man.

There are interesting parallels between houses, storage objects, and instruments at Bafodea. Traditional houses are circular in plan, and most traditional musical instruments appear circular or curvilinear, whether flutes, drums, or idiophones. Most traditional storage objects consisted of circular baskets. Modern houses are rectangular, with square and rectangular rooms, and recent large wooden storage boxes take the same form. The kunkuma lamellaphone and the kututeng, in its metal box, are both rectangular. This suggests a consistent change in musical instruments, living quarters, and storage objects—a hint, perhaps, that neither the kunkuma nor the kututeng, at least in its present form, is very old at Bafodea, and that changing spatial relationships there have been significant. The Bafodea world is becoming a more angular one, and the two lamellaphone forms are part of this change.

Marehu's Views on Music

Marehu is more articulate than Sayo or Muctaru, giving off a greater air of confidence. One day he says to me that if you hear a musician playing any instrument, whether he beats well or not depends upon how he was taught the music. "If you bear it up to your master, you will play well," he claims. I point out that many musicians at Bafodea are self-taught, having learned largely by themselves. "But," he says, "there are few musicians who do not have masters—who do not learn when young, imitating their father or older persons." This is what I have learned about Bafodea musicians, as well as about other professionals here: they like to *say* they were self-taught, that they have "just picked it up." This seems to increase their own conception of themselves and to project it on others. It is an aspect of Bafodea-style craftsman's independence to talk this way.

It is true that except for blacksmiths, diviners, some medicine specialists, and men trained to catch witches, there is no formal apprenticeship system, no art-producing workshop culture, no working for some years with a specialist. This is certainly the case for, among others, musicians, weavers, dancers, singers, traditional tailors, those who make beaded objects (Ottenberg 1983, 1992), hair stylists, and people who do skin decorations. They have only models whom they imitate and perhaps occasionally question or work with. Training is informal and short term, without an apprentice-master relationship. The relative simplicity of many Bafodea crafts and skills allows for this informal learning approach (Ottenberg n.d.). Even where there is a long apprenticeship, like the seven years or so for blacksmiths, much of the time the student is not being taught but is simply working for and observing his master. In the family, learning is largely gender related: sons learn from fathers, daughters from mothers.

Marehu goes on to say that *ato hana,* "knows beat," is the expression for one who beats well, though others use *batohana,* "a fine musician." One who does not beat well, regardless of instrument, is *nde toyeta hana.* "Beating poorly is like a young baby beating a pan," Marehu says. "It is not interesting to people. But the baby beats anyhow!" A good musician beats regularly and people will come around; they will say he knows how to beat the kututeng (*ahan kututeng*). It does not have to be loud or strong, but it has to be steady. I had an American visitor who sings choral music listen to various Bafodea musical forms. She was struck most by how steadily the musicians kept the beat for long periods of time. Another Bafodea man said that beating well means doing so for both singing and dancing. Well-played music is also called *ayere* ("pleasurable"), as in *ayere kututeng.*

"A good kututeng player should know a lot of beats," Marehu says. He cannot explain what these different beats are to me (but see Davenport 1984), and he says they do not have names, although he later classifies general types of Kututeng music for me. He re-iterates the importance of knowing a variety of beats. It is also important, he says, to keep the tongues in their places and to know how to shake and knock the box—*ayutun kututeng* ("shake-kututeng"). Beating the box with the fingers of the right hand is important, he claims. When he does this he continues to play the tongues with his left, carrying the melody and beat with that hand. It is important to know how to sing. He does not know of any good kututeng player who cannot sing, even though he sings little himself. He would not consider one who did not sing to be a good Kututeng musician.

In the Kunkuma group, Marehu says, a good player is one whose beat stays with the others. In the ensemble, the metal U-bar and the kunkuma lamellaphone have only one basic style of beat, found also in Poro music and even in the kututeng, though I have heard embellishments on that beat with this last instrument. In Kunkuma, if someone comes out to dance, the kunkuma player, who is often the lead instrumentalist, adjusts the speed of the beat to the dancer's movements, but it is still the same beat. This pro-cedure for dancing is the same in Poro as well, Marehu says, with the nkali taking the lead in adjusting to the dancer, and I believe it to be true in general for music and dance at Bafodea. Although Marehu cannot see, he can adjust to the dancers when playing the kunkuma since he hears their steps. But he admits that because he is blind the dancers tend to follow him.

Marehu and the Kunkuma Ensemble

Marehu claims that he likes to play the kututeng more than the kunkuma because it was the first instrument he learned. "The sound is sweet" ("mena yame timo"), he says. "People will say it is nice to hear." At least to my Western ear, the kunkuma seems to have a flat tonal quality, perhaps because its tongues are flat and wide, or perhaps because of the large size of the resonator. And with only three tongues, it is less versatile or melodic than the kututeng. It is employed more as a percussion instrument, although it is plucked and not struck. You can make a variety of sounds with the kututeng, Marehu says, which you cannot do with the kunkuma. The latter, never played alone, is not interesting without the metal U-bar or other instruments, he adds, but the kututeng without the U-bar is, to which I agree. When the kututeng player joins the Kunkuma ensemble, his instrument is often drowned out, its subtleties lost, in the clanging of the U-bar, the deep sounds of the kunkuma, and the voice of the singer. So Marehu prefers to play the kututeng alone rather than play any of the Kunkuma instruments in ensemble. Yet he is a member of one.

Marehu shows me his kunkuma. It is nineteen inches long, twelve and a half inches wide, and six and a half inches deep, made of thin pieces of wood nailed together. It has three tongues in the center and a circular hole over their playing side. It is undecorated. The few of these instruments I have seen at Bafodea have also been without design; the box is always of wood, the tongues of metal. The tongues are old hacksaw blades, as is common, so they are wider and flatter than those of the kututeng. Marehu holds the box with both arms, its back against his chest, angled with the finger ends toward him, not away from him as with the kututeng. He plays the tongues with his left hand — from his perspective, the left tongue with his third finger and the middle and right tongues with his second finger. He does not use his thumb as he does in kututeng playing. The tongues in his box are arranged so that the longest (lowest sounding) is on his right, the next longest is in the middle, and the shortest is on the left. On some boxes they are in reverse order, and some musicians play with the right hand instead (fig. 19). The two longest tongues, that is, the lowest sounding, are played the most, Marehu says. Occasionally kunkuma players sit on the playing-tongue end of the box and perform from that position. Van Oven (1973-74:83) writes that the kongoma (kunkuma) sounds like drumming and in Sierra Leone is sometimes employed when drums are not available, but at Bafodea it is not used in this manner.

Marehu knocks the wood on the back of the kunkuma's right narrow edge with a small, crumpled tomato paste tin held in his right hand. This is done commonly, if not with some object then with the open hand alone. The box has a strip of cloth tied to it which the player can put around his neck to hold the instrument to his chest; this is certainly helpful if he performs standing, which is often the case in the Kunkuma ensemble. Some players, however, hold the box on one shoulder, especially if the ensemble is moving. There are no pebbles inside the instrument and no projecting buzzer. It is, in effect, a large and somewhat clumsy kututeng with limited musical possibilities. Even those are not fully exploited, because only one style of beat is usually played on it. What varies is the hitting of the box on its side.

Marehu's metal U-bar (kongole), which van Oven says Limbas generally call *kukotor* (1973-74:83, 1981:24), a term not common among the Limbas at Bafodea, is typical in form. It is about three-fourths inch thick, eight inches long, and five inches across and is played with a thin iron rod some seven inches long (fig. 19). It is often held at shoulder height in the left hand, by the curved section, with its free ends pointing toward the ground. The right hand grips the metal rod at one end and moves it back and forth inside the U-bar, striking both sides in a set beat. The left hand moves the U-bar up and down, holding it at the top of its curve, which makes for a very slight frequency variation in its sound. Both sides of the instrument are the same length.

People who play the kongole say it is physically tiring. To me, after hearing it played steadily for a while in the Kunkuma ensemble, it sounded boring and even annoying, but Bafodeans do not seem to think so. In terms of sound, it is the dominant instrument in the Kunkuma ensemble. The kunkuma is duller and not so pressing to the ear. The metal U-bar is sometimes simply taken from the U-bolt spring support of a lorry or Land Rover. At other times it is fashioned by a blacksmith from a straight bar of European iron or steel. It is not tuned, just prepared to about the right length. So far as I can tell, what is important in playing it is the beat, not its specific frequency.

Marehu's role in the Kunkuma ensemble in town is varied, as the group itself sometimes is, and he is not always asked to play with it. If another kututeng player is not substituted, they just do without one. Once, during an event in honor of a national political figure from the chiefdom who returned to Bafodea Town for a visit—a time when many musical groups appeared—a Kunkuma ensemble came out to play voluntarily. It soon attracted a small crowd of men and women who danced in a circle around the musicians in a slow, shuffling movement, two small steps leading with the right foot and then two with the left as they moved forward a bit. Marehu had his kututeng with him but was not playing a great deal with the group. His friend Salifu Mansaray led the singing. Another friend, Brema Kamara, a Christian Limba diviner from the chiefdom of Kasonko who came to Bafodea years ago with knowledge of Kunkuma music and the kunkuma, played that instrument. Another man was striking an empty metal flask of military design with a metal rod, and there were two U-bar players. In this group, the kututeng would have been lost in the noise of the other instruments, and I think Marehu realized it and so did not play much. The music seemed not to allow for Marehu to come in solo now and then, and indeed, it is unusual for any instrument to be played solo in the Bafodea ensembles.

Just before I left Bafodea I invited the same group to play at my house. Marehu stood in the center of my parlor (it was raining), playing the kututeng with the dancing circle around him. His friend Pari Kamara played the kunkuma while moving in a circle in the dancers' line or while sitting on one end of the kunkuma box in the center of the group. Salifu Mansaray again played the U-bar, either standing in the center or moving in the dance line. There was another U-bar player, and Brema Kamara again struck the metal flask. Salifu, Pari, and the other players each led songs at times. After a while, a neighbor of mine, Suma Mannio Mansaray, whom I have mentioned before in connection with Warana music and dance, came and took over one of the U-bar instruments for a time, and later Marehu's kututeng. Then Marehu stood about for a few minutes and took the kunkuma while Pari moved to one of the iron U-bars. Still later, Brema went from the metal flask to the kututeng for a period of time (figs. 25, 26). Such shifting of instruments among the group is common at Kunkuma performances: except for the kututeng, the instruments appear to be easy to play. What fewer people can do well is to sing the Kunkuma songs skillfully.

Other percussion instruments can be added readily to this kind of ensemble. At one Kunkuma session I heard a man striking a tortoise shell with the working end of a long metal door key. Another time, the Kunkuma group that Marehu played in added on a small wooden nkali, and on another occasion, a man striking the bottom of an iron stirrup with an iron rod. I even heard a group from Kadanso village performing at Kakonso village with two U-bar gongs and two kunkumas playing at the same time. In any case, the usual Kunkuma instruments involve metal, and the whole ensemble has a metallic quality to it—appropriate for a relatively modern musical form, although iron is old in the Bafodea area.[1]

Most Bafodea Limba ensembles are made up entirely of percussion instruments, with the melodic line carried by the voice. The Kunkuma ensemble is exceptional in including the kututeng, but because of its optional character and its relatively weak sound, Kunkuma groups often follow the same pattern as other ensembles. The flute and the kututeng, the only true Limba melodic instruments at Bafodea, are not by accident the only two instruments played primarily alone in a musical world dominated by percussion. At the same time, at least some singing is considered

---

1. Side 1, item 15, of the cassette tape accompanying van Oven's *An Introduction to the Music of Sierra Leone* (1981) is an example she recorded of a Limba Kunkuma-style group playing in Freetown. This group includes the kututeng, kunkuma, hukenken, and kongole, as they are called at Bafodea, or respectively, kututen, kongoma, ken-ken, and kukotor, as she calls them in Freetown.

essential to Bafodea musical ensembles so that a melodic line is present (Nketia 1974:111–15). It is the contrastive and complementary quality of the melodic voice and the percussive instrumentality that gives Bafodea music some of its charm and delightfulness.

I recorded Marehu playing on Brema's eleven-prong kututeng (fig. 27) with a Kunkuma group in March 1979. Marehu sat on a low stool, playing bent over his instrument, which was flat on the floor. Pari Kamara was on the kunkuma, sitting and holding it flat on his lap (it is the most versatile of Bafodea instruments in terms of what position it can be held in). Seri Konteh was on the U-bar. Marehu's friend Salifu Mansaray sang, but he was not feeling well and so another man, Sama, also vocalized. This is the main Kunkuma group in Bafodea Town and its environs, although there are a few other people around who know how to play the kunkuma and occasionally organize another ensemble. My porch was crowded with people; there was singing from the crowd, but it was too close to dance there.

Marehu very much enjoys playing with the group (he never sings with a Kunkuma ensemble but leaves it to stronger voices). He feels a sense of comradeship with his friends that is good for a blind and occasionally lonely man. After the group ended, he commented that even though his eyes were bothering him he could have played all night; he was clearly excited. People found the songs most enjoyable, thought many of them humorous, and relished hearing them as each was repeated over and over again. Here was a case where people seemed quite conscious of the words.

SINGER   ye yaya eyo namandone
          Yes, my mother, how will I settle? [whenever you go to
          settle somewhere, conditions must be right. You
          must have a wife, cloth, things like that]

          a do nonda namandone, yayame tanoko yayamaye
          How will I settle for ever? My mother-in-law, I am here

[a man talking—his wife has left him and he is angry
about it—is one possible interpretation of this line]

Now Salifu sings a popular Poro song:

SALIFU   waliyeee mandenki teme yamayebe
Thank you, the arrangement fits me

CHORUS   salina, mampama, salina, yantiye wiete
Put for me a bit of wine, put for me a bit. I have drunk
a little [this refers to an arrangement with someone,
probably lovers]

SALIFU   yan kponkoiwo yankaho yandi bohiya metiban
I have talked and I have tried. Please hold the town

CHORUS   yayamai
Let me be in peace

SALIFU   kalena bine eh kalena bine, walibenaye badeni ye
eyoooyeooo
Thank you, thank you, I say thanks to married men
[he is thanking men for being patient with their wives.
Married men have so many problems, wife trouble,
etc.]

CHORUS   ye eyoooyeooo
Yes, oh yes, oh yes

SALIFU   yerimowo ba kampara tononi nkala indikoto nande
tonokeba
A woman is jealous [possibly of her husband's other
wives], tie a rope on her so that she will know she has
met a man

CHORUS   ye, eyooo yeooo
Oh yes, oh yes, oh yes

SALIFU   konankondiyeya nakende yan kaselaye ye yan
I will explain that the time I went to Sela

CHORUS   kupahu toko
Oh yes, my trousers were burned [Sela is a Limba
chiefdom west of Bafodea. Paul Hamidu conjectures
that maybe the man was caught with someone's wife
and spent money to beg forgiveness from her husband
(i.e., "burned his trousers")]

SALIFU   yeye o ka madenki ma kpakubeme o yampeye kamende
Yeye [man's name], yes, the arrangement of the chief,
I have agreed to that
CHORUS   sokundayi hoyahele tolontolon sokundayi
It is your business, myself, play, play, your business
Salifu [he has agreed to abide by the chief's law. It is his
business, so let's play music. This is one of the very rare
references to politics in Kunkuma or Kututeng songs]

SALIFU   una dunkuma kanu
This is what God gave me
CHORUS   kumboya awaye kumboya
Trouble, go ahead, trouble

Many Kunkuma and Kututeng songs can be interpreted in a
number of ways according to the listener's sense and experience,
and this last is one of them. Fatamata interprets it to mean that
playing music is the work God gave him (the singer). Paul Hamidu
thinks it means that the Lord gave him trouble and the trouble
will continue — that he is singing, "Let the trouble go ahead, that is
what the Lord gave me." Such room for free interpretation, rather
than having a strictly guided text, is characteristic of many of the
songs at Bafodea (Ottenberg 1989b). There seems to be no "correct" interpretation.

Although people generally dance counterclockwise in a circle
at this and like performances, individuals may come to the center
and dance in livelier steps. Dancing for Kututeng and Kunkuma
is not rigidly governed, perhaps because children may be involved
as well as adults, and perhaps because in the society as a whole,

while standards of skill exist, a great deal of individual variation is allowed. Just as there is variation in dance, so there is in Kututeng playing and its songs. Bafodeans seem to enjoy this sense of freedom in music and dance. They do not expect rigid conformity in the arts except in conjunction with secret society activities, and certainly not in musical forms such as Kututeng and Kunkuma that are not tied to major rites. This freedom is consistent with the variable interpretations of the song texts.

The group quality, the homely social commentaries, the music and dance, and the palm wine all lend a pleasant air to Kunkuma music. Marehu and others enjoy it greatly. Salifu sometimes makes up new songs to the same instrumental music, but mostly this group plays and sings old Kunkuma and Poro songs. Salifu's group has been playing together for some six years and they play well (*ato yerina,* "knows to play"), Marehu says. He adds that they play well from the time they start the performance. "You do not need a warm up," he says, "but you need a crowd to sing in order to play well." There is only one dance, he admits, the same as for Poro music.

Marehu's Kututeng Performance

In June 1979, some eight months after I first met him, I recorded Marehu on the kututeng. He sat on a low stool on my porch with an eleven-tongue instrument borrowed from his friend Brema on the floor. There was only a small crowd, who clapped. They did not sing, perhaps because few people were there, perhaps because Marehu's traditional manner of playing did not attract them, and probably because he is not a strong singer like Sayo. As his friend and fellow musician Salifu Mansaray says about vocal music in general, a good singer (*batosona*) should have a strong voice and the words should be clear, otherwise the crowd will drift away, perhaps to other musicians if any are about. Other Bafodeans made similar comments to me. The clarity of the words seems to be important for aesthetic reasons. Singing at Bafodea, in contrast to kututeng playing, tends to be loud, like Sayo's, and to lack delicate variation.

Figure 25. Brema Kamara showing how he sits with his kututeng *resting on a chair.*

Figure 26. Brema Kamara playing his kututeng, *showing finger positions.*

Figure 27. Brema Kamara's eleven-prong kututeng.

Marehu's singing voice is low and weak. He is often praised for his instrumental abilities but not for his vocalizations.

In this nighttime recording session Marehu sang a little at the beginning and only a few songs later on, but to me his playing seemed developed and brilliant. It grew in intensity and in its beat as he went on. Davenport (1984:chapter 12) confirms that Marehu is the best kututeng player among the three discussed in this book. Earlier, Marehu had said that anything I had for him to drink would please him: the palm wine I obtained certainly did. Afterward I played the tapes of his music over for him and he was very content. "Now I know I can play well!" he said, as if surprised at his own skill. He added that the music sounded the way he wanted it to. Later, quite pleased, he bought himself a wool hat and a sleeping mat with some of the money I paid him.

After some warm-up Tenkele playing, Marehu began. All his songs that night were Kututeng, not Kunkuma or Poro, he said.

yaniobeye marehu woyo yamiobeye mayagawoya
They have done something to me, Marehu, and they have done something to me, not showing off [they have done something to me by making me blind. If I were not blind I would be showing off, but since I am blind I do not show off]

The song was repeated a number of times. Going over the tapes later, Paul Hamidu said that if you have sickness such as blindness or leprosy, you will sing a lot about yourself. Fatamata added that a woman who does not have a good marriage sings like this at the women's Bondo society musical occasions.

Marehu next begins to sing a genre of Kututeng songs that have no special name other than Kututeng, unlike Warana and Tindotin, and that are not associated with a specific dance. Marehu simply considers them to be Kututeng songs and music, not derived from Kunkuma or Poro music.

Then for a while he goes on to another phrase of the song he had begun with:

benkotende marehu woyo
You have seen how Marehu is [referring to his blindness]

Then he returns to the first line—these two are obviously related
in content—and later sings another song so low that we never
obtained the words. Then he goes back to the first line again, followed by solo playing on his instrument.

After this Marehu imitated the xylophone (balanji) on his kututeng—an ideal imitation because the xylophone is very melodic
(Lamm 1968:66–69, fig. 27; Staub 1936:plate 18, fig. 7/8; van Oven
1981:14–16).² He had heard balanji music often in the past. The
small lamellaphone in Africa seems ideal for imitating the music of
other instruments. We have seen how Muctaru does this as well.
Schaeffner (1951:52) mentions that among the Kissi of Guinea, performers on this instrument imitate *banga,* a string instrument, and
Andrew Tracey (1961:45) writes that the Zimbabwean Shona mbira
player Jege A. Tapera "mimics humorously the music of other
ethnic groups."

Chief Yansu Kamara, the late head of the former Limba chiefdom of Kamuke, now the northern part of Bafodea chiefdom,
used to visit Bafodea Town, staying in Marehu's neighborhood
and bringing xylophone musicians with him, whom Marehu used
to hear. It is said that at his home at Sirekude village, this chief
had as many as twelve xylophone players, mainly Mandingos
(fig. 28). During my research, the Bafodea Paramount Chief occasionally hired balanji players for some special event (fig. 29). Xylophone music is generally of Mandingo origin in the Bafodea area,
although it is also played by Yalunka and Kuranko musicians there.
Balanji musicians are particularly hired by Bafodea Muslims, and
the instrument is associated with the introduction of Islam into

2. See Jean Jenkins, "Xylophone Music of the Karanko [*sic*] People" (1979,
side B, no. 4, [discography]), for an example of a sixteen-bar balanji playing at
a wedding ceremony in Kuranko country, east of Bafodea. Also playing are a
double iron idiophone (hukenken), a wooden nkali idiophone, and a double
membrane drum (probably a huban type).

the chiefdom (Ottenberg 1986, 1988b). The music and the religion appear closely associated at Bafodea, although the purer forms of Islam, of course, do not encourage music of this style. Marehu had heard much music from diverse cultures, including Yalunka and Kuranko musicians playing various musical forms, while staying in the multiethnic city of Kabala for medical treatment for his eyes. But at that time he did not pay much attention to their music; he was not interested, he says.

Kubik (1980a), drawing on A. M. Jones (1964:33-34), states that in some areas of Africa where both kututeng-type instruments and the xylophone are found, they are linked by common terminology and the former are considered by people to be smaller, portable versions of the latter. This is clearly not true at Bafodea, nor does Andrew Tracey (1972) think that it is generally so in Africa. At Bafodea the terms for these two instruments differ, and the kututeng probably spread there from the south or southwest of Sierra Leone, as we have seen, while the xylophone is northern in origin, coming from countries beyond Sierra Leone.

Marehu's imitation of the xylophone is skillful and easy to recognize, despite the fact that at Bafodea the xylophone generally has a greater number of sounding boards than does the eleven-tongue kututeng he is playing. In this example, Marehu played in four-beat pentatonic style (Davenport 1984:133-37).

Then Marehu went on to another Kututeng song:

nalungbo nangbuye ketonda dawunte
You have so many lovers, remain with one

Later, my two field assistants and Pastor Kabba of the Wesleyan church at Bafodea laughed as they heard this on tape. They wondered whom he was addressing when he sang. Their reaction suggests that it might have been me, for I was, at the time, a bachelor with a certain reputation—but I was hesitant to press for identification! The suggestion is that Kututeng songs, and perhaps Kunkuma and Poro ones as well, may be directed toward someone

listening but without naming them, perhaps even giving the name
of some other person.

Then, after a break, Marehu sings another Kututeng song:

nandoye tondono yan botoyaha kayike
When I sit so long I will pull my head and go
["I will pull my head and go" (*yan botoyaha*) means to save yourself
from something. I had thought it meant that Marehu was tired
and wanted to go home, but no, as usual, the reference is to lovers.
After you, a man, have been waiting a long time to gain entrance
to some woman, you withdraw]

Then:

akorokonan yan nyietuke mahe
I reveal my mind out, I was about to die last year
[from failing to gain someone's love. The reference is to the
preceding song, one of the few times when there seems to be
direct continuity between songs in Kututeng or Kunkuma]

Another song:

kulongkpon ka ma kika yan makan tete
Love is not like a cloth. [If so] I would get it on credit

Marehu explains that this line means that women are not like cloth,
which, if you do not have money, you can still get on credit from
the seller. You cannot do that with a woman. Paul Hamidu goes
on to say that it is very difficult for poor men to gain a woman's
interest: you need to have good things for her. So it is, he conjectures, for Marehu.

Note that although Marehu considers all these to be Kututeng
songs, and their instrumental playing probably is, the songs' contents are very similar to Kunkuma and Poro verses. The similarity
suggests that this type of text, with its considerable emphasis on
lovers and their problems, is old at Bafodea but has been reinforced

by the introduction of ensemble songs. Note also that Marehu here sings of his personal misfortune, as Sayo did to a much greater extent, suggesting that this too is a traditional form, although Sayo's implementation of it appears to be unique.

In some of his later songs Marehu did not play his kututeng while he sang, but only between the lines. When he did play and sing simultaneously, as in his first and last songs, I could not understand the words properly and failed to get the texts. This performance focused heavily on Marehu's instrument, not on his voice or on a chorus's singing, clearly differentiating him from Sayo and Muctaru.

Marehu's Kututeng Music Classification

At the end of May 1980, not long before I was to leave, I asked Marehu to go over his different kinds of music on the kututeng and classify them. He berated me for not asking him earlier, when we were discussing his music in depth, but he finally agreed. Although this made for an artificial performance setting, it brought out the considerable range of Marehu's skills. (On my return trip in 1988, he told me that he does not plan ahead of time to play pieces at a performance in any definite order. This seems also to be true of Sayo and Muctaru, though if dozens of performances by a particular musician were analyzed, I believe there would be some underlying order to them.)

Marehu sits on my porch in his characteristic manner and starts, using Muctaru's nine-tongue kututeng. I feel that he would rather simply play what he wishes to and not organize things for me, but he is patient and pleasant about it. For once, I quiet the children about us so I can hear him play as well as possible and record him.

He begins with Tenkele music, as is often the case. Then he goes on to categorize and play the following eight types of music.

1. *Maloko.* He has never heard anyone else at Bafodea play this form of Kututeng music, which he indicates derives from the Lokko people, nor have I. He has heard it on the radio in Bafodea

Town a number of times. He does not sing to it but hums softly. Normally people dance in a circle to it at Bafodea, though Maloko differs in rhythm from Kunkuma and Poro, to which people dance in a similar manner. Paul Hamidu told Peter Davenport (1984:127) that the Lokko, although a much smaller group than the Limba, are better known for kututeng playing than are the Limba; a good deal of Lokko music is played on the national radio. Referring to Marehu's Maloko playing, Davenport (1984:127) states that it "is another example of Marehu's creative ability to introduce a melodic idea and to alter it so radically that it is almost lost. Constant references back to pieces of the initial idea, however, maintain a sense of unity and development." In one melodic motif he has twenty variants (Davenport 1984:125–29).

2. *Warana*. This form is the only traditional Kututeng music played by all three of the blind musicians I studied. Marehu sings what he says are just sounds that he made up to go with it — "titilona bila fota" — and later he just hums. Davenport (1984:73–74) indicates that when Marehu plays Warana, he has many more variants than either Sayo or Muctaru, again an indication of his considerable instrumental skill. He is "far more exploratory with the kututeng instrument itself," making use of "inversion, augmentation, diminution, retardation and acceleration techniques" (Davenport 1984:74). Much the same can be said of Marehu's Kututeng music in general.

3. *Yegbile*. This traditional Kututeng music has only one song, according to Marehu, words he made up (though Paul Hamidu believes that the words, like the instrumental music, are old).

yan niobeye kanu naniberine
They have done something to me; I will cry to the Lord

This is a kind of line we have heard before from Marehu, as well as from Sayo. Marehu indicates that normally Yegbile is played at Bafodea without singing and has a specific dance in which one arm goes forward and the other backward. Anyone who feels like it can do it. I never saw it danced at Bafodea, and I do not think it is common; neither Sayo nor Muctaru played it for me (Davenport 1984:84–88).

4. *Kukangtan.* Like Muctaru, Marehu plays this second funeral ensemble music on the kututeng. He performs some preparatory Tenkele and then the Kukangtan music, without song, imitating at times the wooden nkali and at other times the women's small samburi drum. According to Davenport (1984:98–101), Marehu plays this music in a variety of closely related patterns.

5. *Kunkuma.* First Marehu pretends that he is playing the three-tongue kunkuma, playing its music with his left hand while striking the box with the fingers of his right, much as he does on the kunkuma itself. He is very skillful at this and the people listening admire his performance. Then he goes on to play the kututeng the way he does as a kututeng player in the Kunkuma ensemble, ending with a sudden bang on his box. He often finishes a piece this way, as Sayo sometimes does, making a sharp break in the music. Davenport (1984:105–10) states that rather than merely repeating a Kututeng pattern as a basic solo with chorus singing, Marehu de-emphasizes the singing (possibly because of his weak voice) and focuses on instrumental proficiency and melodic exploration.

6. *Balanji.* This xylophone-style music, as played by Marehu, has been discussed earlier. I have to note the delight Marehu takes in imitating other musical forms and instruments from Balanji to Maloko, Kukangtan, and Kunkuma. This suggests that he has a keen ear for music. (Figs. 28 and 29.)

7. *Maharasi.* I had never heard of this traditional Kututeng music until Marehu played it. He hums, but there are no words. Men and women dance to it, he says, not in a line but putting one foot forward, then back, then the other foot forward and back, dancing in place. This seems to be something like the dancing of Kuberiberi, which Muctaru plays, but the instrumental aspect differs (Davenport 1984:92). Marehu says it is a dance that was done to the kututeng in the old Bafodea Town. Young men liked it a lot, but it is not performed any more.

8. He gives his last category of music no special name; it is simply Kututeng. He plays a variety of pieces and says he is just

Figure 28. Yele Seku, a Mandingo balanji *musician at Telia in the old Kamuke chiefdom, now the northern part of Bafodea.*

Figure 29. Mandingo musicians playing the xylophone, balanji, *at a second funeral ceremony at Kadanso village.*

playing the instrument (*ayeren kututeng*). Then he pauses on the instrument and sings:

tono namokondo tukumahologoyi
Mother-in-law, don't listen to what people say, my heart is bad
[people are talking about me, but do not listen to them,
I am angered about that]

Marehu says this is not Kunkuma or Poro, just a song. In fact, he considers it to be Kututeng music. Then he sings another song in this genre, with playing, the song about "love is not like a cloth." Finally, he returns to Yegbile music, and this ends the session. He claims he does not know the "lizard" music—Kuberiberi, or Kpunkimadada—that Muctaru plays, or Tindotin, which both Sayo and Muctaru play, although he can play Tindotin on the flute. This suggests that Kuberiberi may not be traditional Kututeng music but relatively new to Bafodea, possibly coming from Kenema, where Muctaru relearned to play the kututeng.

Like Muctaru, but unlike Sayo, Marehu has a wide repertoire of categories of music, though in the times I heard him play without my direction he performed mainly traditional Kututeng forms, especially Warana and one or two other types. His classification of Kututeng music, unlike the classification I created for Sayo's music, is based on differences in playing the instrument and not on song texts.

In his love of variations, the complexity of his playing, and his delight in imitating—features well recognized by people at Bafodea—Marehu is the most skillful kututeng instrumentalist of the three musicians discussed here. His focus on the instrument rather than on his voice is consistent with his playing primarily traditional Kututeng music, which he knows from living in the old Bafodea Town. Why are these forms less seldom played in the new town? It may be because of missionary influence, for the new town was the center of American Wesleyan Methodist missionary activity in the chiefdom for some years after it was settled. The missionaries helped bring in outside influences of all kinds, including choral singing in church. Also, the town is the focus of changes in the chiefdom, including new forms of music such as Kunkuma, Poro, and Rainbow. Probably both factors are involved.

On my brief return to Bafodea Town in 1988, I asked Marehu to play, and I have already mentioned how Sayo came in and took over from him. At this session Marehu played with the same skill as before. I am reminded of what Nketia (1974:81) has written: "A simple-looking *mbira* may be quite a sophisticated instrument in terms of its technical demands." Marehu has mastered these demands very well.

In 1988 I noticed for the first time that when Marehu plays sitting, or even occasionally when standing, he moves largely with his fingers and arms while the rest of his body is quiet. Even his arm movements seem limited. In this style Marehu contrasts with Sayo, who cannot keep still, moves his whole body as he plays, and often rises to move about and even dance a bit when performing, shuffling his feet with his body bent somewhat forward at the waist. My notes comment that "Pa Sayo is all heart, Marehu technique." It is not that Marehu is a cold person or performer but rather that he is in closer control of his emotions than Sayo, whose personal feelings seem so much to need expression in his performances.

At another meeting with Marehu in 1988, he revealed that he has a favorite piece that he says he made up, which he had never played for me before—unless I simply missed it, which is certainly possible. He refers to the piece as *sumbutanken*, a term that means "grass cutter–rice," and as he plays it he grumbles a phrase, "Oh sumbutanken pakalaba," making the instrument's tongues grumble as well. The phrase means that an animal called the grass cutter finishes the rice. This animal, a field rodent of persistent trouble to farmers because it devours the ripening rice, is also good meat to eat. It is caught in traps set at the edges of the low-fenced fields. It is because of the grass cutters and the birds, which also eat the rice, that boys go to the farms at ripening time to chase the birds away with slingshots and to trap the grass cutters, just as earlier in the year they go to help with planting. Marehu now tells me that in either case, when they return from the farms they drink palm wine, and if the moon is showing they call out a Kututeng player and dance Warana to see who is the strongest. Their girl friends, who are there as well, will not dance, but admire them. Even at the farms, boys may play the kututeng for amusement, so Marehu's *sumbtaken* music has direct associations with the kututeng.

Marehu says his instrument has nothing to do with God, ancestors, or sacrifices. "No, it is just the music that people want played," he tells me. He never uses charms to assist his playing. This is clearly a secular music and instrument, although one that women do not play. There is no law against their playing it, he says, it is just the custom.

In the winter of 1992 I learned by mail from a Bafodea man in Freetown that Marehu had passed away. All three of the musicians met in this book are now gone. They brought joy to many through their music, which also brought them happiness, sociability, and friendship.

6 The World of Three Kututeng Musicians

Performance is a means by which people reflect on their current condition, define and/or re-invent themselves and their social world, and either reinforce, resist or subvert prevailing social orders. —Margaret Thompson Drewal, *"The State of Research on Performance in Africa"*

SAYO, MUCTARU, AND MAREHU WERE ALL OF MATURE AGE, blind, wifeless, childless, without farms, hungry at least some of the time, poor, and dependent upon relatives for food and housing. None of the three begged for a living in the usual sense of the term, as I have seen blind people doing on the streets of Freetown and in the United States. Indeed, I never met such a beggar in the chiefdom. None of these musicians had a boy to lead him about, as is characteristic of blind West Africans in some other areas, whether musicians or not. This lack of a guide was particularly surprising for Sayo, who traveled from community to community.

The three were the major Kututeng musicians in the Bafodea Town area, including nearby Sakuta, where Sayo lived. Each performer brought his own particular skills and experience to his music, which was well enjoyed by others, even if sometimes in different ways. The musicians attracted not only children but also some adults of both sexes to their performances. All three enjoyed a good drink and sociability, despite being lonely at times because of their blindness. To varying degrees, each played other instruments as well as the kututeng in ensembles—Muctaru only very occasionally, however. All three had had some experience outside of the chiefdom, and all three were conscious of being Limbas and Bafodeans. Because few people in Bafodea could read and write (there was only one small primary school in the entire chiefdom when I carried out research there), the lack of these abilities in the blind musicians was not the dramatic loss it would have been in the more reading-oriented West.

The kututeng instrument on which they performed is relatively easy to carry, in contrast with the heavier and more awkward huban, kunkuma, and nkali, and not physically difficult for blind persons to play. It is an instrument associated with children and with the musicians' own childhood, and thus with life's continuity. All three played the kututeng at least to some extent before going blind; none of the three was blind from birth. All chose to play whenever possible rather than do nothing, unlike other blind people in the chiefdom except for an occasional sightless mat maker.

All, then, had in music a public outlet for their talent and for their emotional feelings, whether they expressed those feelings directly, as Sayo did, or indirectly, like Marehu. Music was a way for these men to handle loneliness and feelings of inadequacy, for it gave them social groups and individuals with whom to interact. It allowed them to see the social world in ways other blind people could not, in pleasant and nonthreatening situations, and it gave them the opportunity to exhibit skill and creativity. Some of their songs suggested destiny. They sang of God's will, of what the Lord had written for them. They sang of troubles, some their own, some affecting others, and also of matters that little touched them: sexual ones—lovers—a world that existed for them largely in song and performance. Singing of these matters brought them into a part of the flow of life that they did not enjoy directly. It kept them human, kept them from being distanced from others, and fed their imaginations.

Status and Children

All three musicians held a triply inferior status. First, although musicians were certainly needed in Bafodea, they occupied a generally low status in a society where big men, important farmers, and persons senior in age usually did not make music. Second, among musicians, the status of Kututeng musicians was low compared with that of other players because their music (like flute music) was associated with childhood and because the players were rarely hired by the Paramount Chief, village headmen, or other important individuals. Kututeng music played a somewhat peripheral rather than a central role in the Bafodea musical scene. This was reflected, I think, in the presence of only two types of lamellaphones at Bafodea, in contrast to the five used among the Shona, for whom this music is more basic and is associated with religious beliefs and rituals (Berliner 1978:29–30).

The third status factor was that of being blind in a society that did little for the sightless beyond minimally feeding, housing, and clothing them. Anything more than that the three musicians accomplished largely on their own; their music was a product of their own egos, their own striving to be useful. Even in Muctaru's case, his learning the kututeng at Kenema was incidental to the training course in basketry and gardening, but he made good use of it.

Cultural orientations at Bafodea discouraged blind people, both men and women, from taking an active role in Bafodea life. To marry, a man needed money. He should also be productive in farm or trade and, in older age, in politics and settling disputes. Blindness, in fact, for at least one of our musicians, was equated with impotence and dependence, which were shameful for men. Because of seasonal workloads in farming, there were periods when men and boys sat around in homes, on porches, or at friends' residences doing little or nothing (women and girls seemed almost always to have household duties, although blind women were handicapped in doing housework as well as in farming). The blind, however, sat longer and more quietly. In a society that stresses activity — and does so much of the year—they lived a life of partial social castration.

For Sayo, Muctaru, and Marehu, there was a strong equation between their blindness and a childlike state, and also multiple associations with children. The blind, like children, were dependent upon others for food, clothing, housing, and some guidance. The music they played was music learned by young children—an early part of Bafodea life experiences. Children made up a substantial part of the audience at Kututeng performances; their enthusiasm and vitality or their lack of it largely determined the quality of the event. In this sense, the three blind musicians did not have fully adult status. They lived in an ambiguous world of both childhood and adulthood. Having no children of their own, they were dependent on the children who were drawn to their music for a part of their musical socializing. This was particularly the case for Sayo and Muctaru; Marehu did not attract children as much. The youngsters who responded to their playing and singing became, for a moment, the musicians' children, fulfilling the desire of every Bafodea man to have his own. Without children, men have little status. The very existence of these Kututeng musicians as adults who in some ways experienced a childlike dependency reinforced the normal (sighted) adult values of maleness in Bafodea society.

The three Kututeng musicians were connected to the larger world through the very act of performing, when each temporarily became part of a larger community of participants, including responders and listeners, which yet did not restrict their individualities as players (Blacking 1973:50–51). Performing was a widening and enriching experience for them in a world in which they had few other expressive outlets. If they rarely or never enjoyed the pleasures of sexual intercourse, then the communications that occurred during a performance—including, of course, those with women—were an important outlet for them vis-à-vis people with whom they might otherwise have had little contact.

Thus the blind Kututeng musician lived in a world of both children and adults. He sang of lovers and of sexuality to an audience of children as well as some adults, yet he also played lizard and monkey-tail dance music for youngsters. He continued to play the kututeng beyond the age when most males did. He was neither a child nor fully an adult, existing between two worlds, not totally of either. Except for the flute, other Bafodea music is primarily for adults, although children may dance about and even sing to it. (Exceptions are the preinitiation dances for adolescents, where older boys and girls play major roles, but even there a good deal of dancing and singing is done by adults.) Yet these three musicians moved farther along the road to adult male status than most sightless people in the chiefdom did, for they had a creative profession, a skill that other blind people lacked, an ability that distinguished them from the others. And both Sayo and Marehu, and very occasionally Muctaru, played in ensembles at times with sighted adult musicians, further allowing them to "see" — to experience their culture.

The equation of adulthood and childhood for these three musicians is even more complex because, although they lacked the full status of adult males in their society, they played fatherly roles as Kututeng players. The Kututeng performer was a surrogate father, for a musical moment in time, to the children who responded to him in singing and dancing — some of whom were regular followers of his in the neighborhood where he lived and played. He played a nonpunishing, supportive role for them. His interactions with them were pleasant and not very demanding, asking only that they respond properly to him and allowing them to suggest further songs to play. The children were free to complain if the instrumentalist put too strong demands on them (as they once did to Muctaru), to simply not sing if they did not like what he was playing, and to leave at will. The musician was a teacher for them. His songs informed them about certain aspects of adult life, and their experience in responding to him formed an aspect of their musical education. The nonhostile father-child relationship inherent in the performance had positive aspects for both musician and children, and the performance was clearly pleasurable to both.

I have elsewhere stressed the importance of the continuity of people's aesthetic experience from childhood to adulthood and how it works to serve positive adult needs and activities (Ottenberg 1982:175–76, 1989b). I believe that this importance holds true for the Kututeng musicians. The association of this music with their childhood was a positive support for them, providing them with a sense of continuity over time, an association with a status they enjoyed before becoming blind, and an entrée into an adult musical skill.

Like sighted musicians, these three Kututeng players were open to the critical evaluations of both children and adults. Some people thought Sayo was a poor kututeng instrumentalist, or that he sang too much of himself, or that drink sometimes weakened his performance. Yet others loved his voice and songs and willingly responded to his music. Some felt that Marehu represented the true Kututeng tradition and was by far the best instrumentalist of the three, but wished he would sing more strongly and more often. Muctaru was particularly loved by children, but even he, at one of his performances, was criticized by some of them for offering songs they had difficulty responding to. Some people felt that Muctaru, in contrast to Marehu, did not really play true Kututeng music but music that was mainly derivative of ensemble forms. Others liked Muctaru's playing very much because the Kunkuma and Poro music he performed on his kututeng and in song were popular at Bafodea. Just as the musicians offered various interpretations of Kututeng music, so their listeners offered varieties of criticisms of their performances. There was clearly no one Kututeng music but a complex range, sometimes personalized, sometimes drawing from the new, and sometimes making good use of tradition.

Though none of the three musicians derived a great deal of public status from his Kututeng music or made much money from this very part-time occupation, some Bafodeans considered Kututeng music to be highly desirable. Zemp (1971:39) has pointed out that a similarly ambivalent low status characterizes the Dan musicians of Ivory Coast, who play a similar instrument. Merriam

(1979) and Ames (1968, 1973a) have noted the same for other parts of Africa and other instruments, as have Becker (1966) and MacLeod (1993) for certain musicians in the United States.

The general lack of status for Bafodea musicians was a consequence of a number of factors. Middle-aged and older people at Bafodea often felt that it was not proper for them to perform music or to take an active part in musical events, although they hired musicians for second funerals, marriages, and other rites. Muslims also were wary of some musicians for violating the Koran with their drinking, their supposed promiscuity at some events, and the texts of some of their songs. Bafodea musicians attracted crowds of both sexes when they performed, sometimes late into the night, and out of this activity sometimes came drunkenness and sexual liaisons. Although the blind Kututeng musicians were not generally seen by others as a threat to womanhood, sighted musicians were sometimes viewed that way, as were men who came to the performances. The crowds at Kututeng performances were often not of high status. Elites rarely appeared at them, and their absence did not encourage a high status for the performers.

Kututeng (like flute music) carried an added burden that other music did not: it was not usually an aspect of ensemble music, although its instrument occasionally appeared in Kunkuma ensembles and even, at times, in Poro ones. Ensembles, however, not individual Kututeng performers, were generally hired for ritual events. The Mansaray clan, the leading clan politically in the chiefdom, from which the Paramount Chief is selected, in theory discouraged its members from becoming musicians; the activity was not fit for leaders. It was expected that musicians should come from the other two main clans, the Konteh and the Kamara. Yet two of our three Kututeng musicians were Mansarays, and so were some of the ensemble players I have mentioned. I have doubts about how strong this pressure to desist really was, except among older Mansarays. In the case of the three blind musicians, it did not appear that there was any pressure against their playing—they were left to do what they could.

Yet in performance these three musicians had status for the

moment. They were in charge, leading the music. From holding low status in the society they became, for brief periods of time, the center of interest in the group gathered around them, even if it was partly made up of children. It is true that chorus members might complain about the songs, refuse to sing, or simply not respond well for some reason. But Stone's (1982:128) characterization of Kpelle music in Liberia holds for Bafodea choruses as well: "Participants relate to one another in hierarchical, interdependent ways with a shifting point-counterpoint relationship typical of event interaction." Despite the subtleties of the interactions that could occur at a performance, the Kututeng musician was in charge. It is also clear that although I paid attention to virtually all varieties of musicians at Bafodea in my research, as well as to people in other art forms in the context of my studies of the aesthetics of ritual, my interaction with these three musicians—asking them to play for me, paying them, and paying attention to them—raised their status to a certain extent, for I was considered to be an influential person at Bafodea. Perhaps, too, it lowered mine as something of a "big man," though I was not conscious of this in the field.

I believe that playing music raised the status of these three musicians in a cultural context where the sightless rarely had any occupation at all and where being a blind musician was not a standard role (almost all musicians have sight). They were admired by some Bafodeans for having a profession and for being publicly active. It may be that the activities of these three musicians changed general attitudes toward the blind in the Bafodea Town area to some degree. I found it difficult to judge this issue.

Song Texts

Being of low status at Bafodea, however, held some advantages for these three musicians. It allowed them to sing publicly and to a certain extent freely about social life, to comment on married women's vagaries and on male sexuality, often in humorous ways, to air the damages wrought by witchcraft, and to make certain kinds of social commentaries on everyday life that were otherwise rarely made in public except during court cases and other disputes. I do not think being blind gave them any extra freedom in this regard over nonblind musicians. We have seen the texts of the Kunkuma songs, for example, sung by people with sight (Ottenberg 1993).

But there were unstated boundaries to this freedom of expression. The Kututeng songs did not attack local political or religious figures. Islam was rarely mentioned except for its God, *ala* (Allah), nor was Christianity, whose God seems never to have been invoked at all. Despite the fact that Muctaru and Marehu were Christians, as were some of their chorus members, all of whom must have heard and probably sung Christian songs in the local Wesleyan Methodist church, Christianity was not an issue in the Kututeng songs. It was not seen as either helpful or harmful with reference to witches, adultery, and death. The traditional Limba God, Kanu, was mentioned in song much in the same way as the Muslim God; sometimes one seemed readily substitutable for the other. The song texts only rarely criticized a person directly, unlike the case of the Okumkpa masquerade among the Afikpo Igbo of Nigeria, which I studied at an earlier time (Ottenberg 1972, 1975:87–143). At Bafodea they occasionally did so indirectly, however. As a rule the songs were not direct attacks on individuals, on any group, or on any religion.

The Kututeng song texts touched on two of several major areas of tension at Bafodea: conflict between a husband and his wife's lover (and also between husband and wife), and witchcraft matters. Bafodea chiefdom was a society in which witchcraft accusations were endemic and where witchcraft beliefs and activities were related to a variety of disputes and hostilities, often involving interfamily and interpersonal tensions. Other major tension zones, including disputes over succession to village headship, land disputes, arguments over the destruction of Limba farmers' crops by Fula-owned cows, and other interethnic matters, seem not to have been within the purview of Kututeng. It is not clear why, although often this latter type of conflict concerned disputes involving large numbers of people, suggesting that Kututeng songs were normally related to issues surrounding smaller-scale social relationships. Perhaps, in the case of those topics not brought up, to have raised the issues would have been to involve powerful social groups in the chiefdom. Stone (1982:130) suggests for the Kpelle of nearby Liberia that "some aspects of culture are more connected to music than others. It is not simply that some of these aspects are reflected and others are not reflected. Rather they are subtly manipulated and toyed with in the context of musical interaction."

Although the kinds of Kututeng song materials that were presented seem clear, within that framework there were varying interpretations of individual song texts on the part of the Kututeng musicians, chorus members, and listeners. This diversity of understanding was accentuated by the brevity of the texts, which sometimes made allusions rather than concrete statements.

One of the attractions of Kututeng, Kunkuma, and Poro music was that it allowed important topics related to deep emotions and anxieties among Bafodeans to be expressed, especially sexual matters, witchcraft, and misfortune. These musical forms also attracted interest because they stood in contrast to the general rules of the political and status establishment, which said, Go to bed early—nighttime is for quiet, rest, and sex at home between spouses. Work hard, drink little, and do not sing publicly of lovers and witches.

Everyday life had a drab quality at Bafodea. Farm work and other labor was hard. The region was not rich in money and only rarely in food. Occasions for public rejoicing came largely in the dry season, from about October to May, when the major rites were carried out. Nevertheless, leaders and prominent persons hired ensembles and allowed periods of freedom of expression surrounding rituals. At some of these rites, however, the songs were not of lovers and witches and misfortune but were specific to the event. The songs of both the boys' and the girls' preinitiation rites, which were conducted separately at Bafodea, were much concerned with parents' loss of their children to the bush and ultimately to adulthood. The songs of marriage rites (Ottenberg 1988a, 1989b) voiced the girl's transition from one household to another and the uncertainties and possible pleasures of marriage. Kututeng, Kunkuma, and Poro were secular musical forms which, if they were played at these kinds of special events at all, were played in secondary performances, so their singers had greater freedom of expression.

Two of Stone's comments (1982:128) on Kpelle music in Liberia are consistent with my view of Bafodea: "Audio communication is a primary means of interpretation in everyday life and in music events," and "other kinds of experience often are translated into sound terms for expression." This raises the issue of whether, in Western societies that rely considerably on the silent printed word, we view musical performances fundamentally differently from the way members of cultures such as Bafodea chiefdom do. (Granted that with the advent of radio, television, and videocassette recorders we are moving back to an audio and audiovisual world.) I do not know the answer.

Another attraction of Kututeng music, of course, was simply that it was pleasurable to Bafodeans. They liked the instrumental playing, usually enjoyed the instrumentalist's voice and what he sang, and took pleasure in participating with others, perhaps with a little drink, during the evening and nighttime. The sheer aesthetics of Kututeng should not be overlooked in the search for the importance or the meaning of the texts and other matters.

Individual Experience and Expression

Despite all three of these Kututeng musicians' playing the same instrument, sharing similar backgrounds, and having many experiences in common, there were marked differences in the way they performed and the kind of Kututeng they played (table 1). This suggests that the study of any single cultural element such as Kututeng as a form of aesthetics and social behavior, without strong reference to individual experience and careers, is likely to fail. Sayo had a strong singing voice but was less skillful on the instrument than the other two. Sorrowful in personal expression, he was the only one of the three to use the recitative to any extent. Muctaru exhibited a balance of kututeng instrumental playing and voice and less rarely projected his personal feelings. Marehu was strong and very skillful as an instrumentalist but weak in voice. He only occasionally projected sorrow, and he employed more dramatic instrumental variations and complexities than either Muctaru or Sayo.[1] Marehu was competent, well controlled, and organized, unlike Muctaru, who covered a wide range of feelings from depression to happiness with an almost childlike smile and who had the closest contact with children of the three — they generally responded well to his musicianship. Sayo was perpetually on the move, partly for his trading activities, but it also seemed to be his nature to keep busy. Muctaru seldom left home, and Marehu traveled about only a little.

In performance, Sayo was often in bodily motion, sometimes standing up and dancing, whereas Muctaru was quiet, sitting on a chair or stool. Marehu was even quieter, liking to sit low on a small stool or even on the floor, with his instrument on the floor as well, where he could strike its front end against the floor from time to time. There was no standard body stance among these three musicians.

Muctaru was a musical loner, rarely playing in ensembles, whereas Sayo played with some groups and used to play with others, and he was once a storyteller — the only one of the three to have been so. Storytellers at Bafodea sometimes play the wooden nkali gong or a drum and also sing at times, with song responses from the audience. Marehu played with a Kunkuma group that did not perform traditional music, but when performing alone, he mainly played the more traditional Kututeng music. Sayo's musicianship was highly personalized and quite innovative, while Muctaru largely performed a kind of Kututeng growing out of Kunkuma and Poro ensemble styles.

---

1. Davenport (1984:196n1) suggests that proficiency in kututeng instrumental playing "apparently refers to the player's ability to play fast passages, to creatively vary a recognizable theme; in general, to hold people's interest through clever transformation of familiar melodic ideas in extended instrumental performances."

Table 1

The Three Kututeng Musicians

	Sayo Kamara
Age at time of study	Middle aged
Age at onset of blindness	Child
Place of residence	Sakuta village
Married? Children?	No, no
Family situation	Apparently supportive
Personality	Assertive, aggressive, on the move
Played kututeng *as a child?*	Yes
When took up kututeng *professionally?*	Very young
Kututeng playing	Least skillful
Singing	Strong, assertive voice, recitative
Song texts	Quite personal, sorrowful, some Poro, Kunkuma texts
Body position when playing	Much in motion, sitting, standing, dancing
Plays in ensembles?	Formerly many forms, then only farm ensemble music
Changes from traditional Kututeng music?	To personalized music, and Poro and Kunkuma music
External musical influences on kututeng *playing?*	Kunkuma and Poro music
Music attracts children?	Yes
Other activities	Trading, formerly a storyteller
Travel	To neighboring villages, Kabala and Dogolaya
Status	Low, but enhanced by being a musician

Table 1 continued

Muctaru Mansaray	Marehu Mansaray
Middle aged	Middle aged
Adult	Adult
Bafodea Town	Bafodea Town
No, no	No, no
Minimal support	Minimal support
Quiet, sometimes depressed	Calm, balanced emotionally
Yes	Yes
Adult	Adult
Skillful	Most skillful
Balanced, singing and playing	Weak voice, mostly playing
Impersonal, largely Poro, Kunkuma texts	Impersonal, little song, some Kututeng texts
Sitting on stool	Sitting on stool, floor
Only very occasionally Kunkuma ensemble	Kunkuma ensemble
To Poro and Kunkuma music	A little change from Kututeng, and plays in Kunkuma ensemble
Kunkuma and Poro music	From radio a little, and plays in Kunkuma ensemble
Yes	Yes
Occasional basket making	A little farming with a friend
Bafodea Town, mainly his neighborhood, lived in Kenema at one time.	Bafodea Town, a little at the farms, lived in Kabala for a time.
Low, but enhanced by being a musician	Low, but enhanced by being a musician

History and Change

The evidence from these three musicians and other sources suggests something of the probable history of Bafodea Kututeng music. The more traditional forms, from the pre-1950s time of the old Bafodea Town, emphasize instrument playing, sometimes solo and at other times accompanied by specific forms of dancing for each musical form, but there is little or no singing. Musician-chorus music is uncommon and limited to a few lines. Traditional Kututeng music is clearly allied with flute melodies and may have derived from them if the kututeng is of later origin than the flute, as is possible. Both instruments stress melody and can be played without song. The more traditional Kututeng music is still characteristic of some rural Bafodea villages.

I surmise that Kututeng music and its instrument probably do not predate the twentieth century, unless there was a now-forgotten wood or calabash form of the instrument. Iron was worked in the Bafodea region before this century, however, as is evidenced by iron slag piles, so that earlier forms of metal resonators might have been produced. If so, despite my interest in Bafodea's material culture, I neither saw nor heard of it. Marehu and other Kututeng players, when they lacked a kututeng, did not consider making or having one made out of wood or a calabash but searched for a gallon tin to take to a blacksmith or other person to fashion the instrument. The same may be true of the instrument's tongues, which seem now always to be of metal. Whether they were of bamboo or other wood at an earlier time at Bafodea is uncertain.

Montandon (1919:39–40, 101, fig. *k*) discusses the earliest form of the lamellaphone that I know of for Sierra Leone, of Temne origin, collected no later than 1917. With sixteen bamboo tongues, a wooden sounding board, and a lozenge-type projection at its far end, it lacks a resonator. This suggests that early Bafodea forms may simply have had the tongues mounted on a board, with no resonator. When metal cans became available, the board and keys were set onto the can to give the instrument a richer sound.

Montandon's sketch of the early Temne example (1919:39, fig. *k*) suggests that the instrument was played with the fingers in the same direction as present-day ones in Bafodea and the rest of Sierra Leone. Montandon (1919:39–40) mentions another, somewhat similar instrument collected by Ankermann from Cameroon. Ankermann's text and figure (1901:33–34, fig. 53) indicate a similar playing position for the instrument as that found today in Sierra Leone. Made of wood, it has a projecting wooden prong at its far end and, like Montandon's Sierra Leone example, no metal pieces attached to form a buzzer. It differs from the latter in having a narrow, hollow wooden resonator. This instrument might represent a prototype for the Bafodea form, as opposed to simply a plain wooden sounding board without a resonator.

What is apparently occurring is a decline in the traditional Kututeng forms, at least in and near the chiefdom capital, and an increase in call-and-response singing and clapping brought about through the influence of ensemble musical forms, particularly Kunkuma and Poro. With these changes have probably come greater adult participation in Kututeng—a shift from its being largely a children's music to its becoming a more mixed child-adult form. As Davenport suggests (1984:152), all three of these musicians, having had outside contacts, "have introduced a more social, less individual use of the kututeng."

The Cultural Structure of Kututeng

By following three musicians and their music, I have worked out a sense of the types of music and their history at Bafodea, what I might call the *cultural structure* of its music, referring back to my discussion of personhood in the first chapter of this book. There are the traditional Kututeng forms—Tenkele, Warana, Kudingpon, Yegbile, and Tindotin—as well as music that Marehu simply calls Kututeng but claims is traditional. Whether Kuberiberi is traditional or not is unclear. Marehu, the traditionalist, did not perform it, although Muctaru did. It has a specific dance form associated with it, like some other traditional Kututeng forms, but

Muctaru's music generally derives from outside Bafodea, and if Marehu did not know it, it may indeed have had an external origin.

Maloko music, which, of the three musicians, only Marehu played, derived from the Lokko people, who also play it in single instrument form. Another class of Kututeng music originated in ensemble music from outside the chiefdom in the last forty years or so. It includes Kunkuma and Poro, widespread in Sierra Leone; Balanji music of Mandingo, Yalunka, and Kuranko origin from sources north and northeast of Bafodea; and Rainbow from urban Freetown and up-country cities and towns.

Then there is the more traditional ensemble music heard at various Bafodea events but carried over to the kututeng instrument: Mankonkoba farm music, Gbondokali boys' preinitiation dance forms, and the second funeral music of Kukangtan. Finally, some music appears to be unique to the individual Kututeng player, including some of Sayo's—especially his recitative style—and Marehu's grass-cutter "grumble" music.

This is a rich corpus of Kututeng, some forms having been played by all three musicians, others by one or two of them.[2] None of them imitated women's music, except for Kukangtan, for which Marehu imitated the beat of the women's small samburi drums. We see a pattern of both the continuation of tradition and the relatively recent adaptation of local ensemble music to Kututeng, as well as a growing influence of outside musical ensembles and musical influences via the radio, the tape recorder, and the city.

Musical Culture, Personhood, Agency, and Structure

If we look at these three major players of Kututeng, all residing in a single geographical and cultural area, it is clear that they were agents re-creating the cultural structure of Kututeng music at Ba-

2. Davenport (1984:53) summarizes most of these musical forms in his table 1, although I have indicated in my text some additions and some doubts about the placement of Kuberiberi.

fodea. This generalization is particularly true for Sayo and Muctaru. The latter's agency lay more in bringing Kunkuma and Poro ensemble styles to Kututeng, while Sayo's lay primarily in his individualistic interpretation of music and song and his employment of recitative. Marehu was less involved in re-creating Kututeng culture than in expressing its more traditional aspects—he was more an agent of musical stability. Nevertheless, he too played the kututeng with a Kunkuma ensemble at times, although much of what he played was drowned out by the other instruments and tended to be simpler in form than the music he performed solo. Kututeng music clearly changed from the years before Bafodea Town moved to its new site in the mid-1950s to the time when I conducted research in 1978–80, and these three musicians played major roles in this process.

Changes in Kukuteng musical structure were in line with the spread of certain popular-culture musical ensemble forms, such as Kunkuma, throughout Sierra Leone. And Sayo represented an increasing musical individualism in the country brought about by general conditions of change. His Kututeng, however, was perhaps less an expression of direct contact with this larger musical-individuality–oriented world than an expression of the way general cultural conditions almost everywhere in Sierra Leone had become more favorable to Sayo's style of performance.

In terms of agency and social structure, Sayo and Muctaru brought about a change in the social relationships of Kututeng performances by emphasizing call-and-response singing and dancing in the Kunkuma and Poro style over the more specialized dancing styles and the lesser emphasis on the voice that went with traditional forms of Kututeng, as practiced by Marehu. Yet Marehu's regular commitment to playing the kututeng with a Kunkuma ensemble suggests that he was not so strictly traditional after all but also enjoyed more contemporary music involving his instrument.

These three musicians were both musical and social actors at Bafodea in the context of their culture and society, which was slowly changing as outside influences made their way to the isolated chiefdom. Viewing them as individuals acting in cultural and social structural fields gives us insights into how they were influenced by those fields and how they altered them.

Personal Experiences

The personal life experiences of these three musicians contributed greatly to both their re-creation of Kututeng popular music and their holding onto its tradition. Marehu sometimes referred to the old town and its music and saw his heritage as lying there. Muctaru's attending a school for the blind to learn basketry and gardening set him on a course toward ensemble-derived Kututeng music. Sayo's personality—strong, active, sorrowful, and demanding of attention—related firmly to the kind of music he evolved.

Childhood factors unknown to me undoubtedly influenced the eventual musicianship of these three men. So must have the particulars of the illnesses that led to their blindness and the types of parents and other family members they had. Sayo, as my colleague Labelle Prussin, who met and heard him, pointed out to me, seemed the most narcissistic, most prone to breakdown (mainly through alcohol), and most likely to cause "palaver" (over money matters)—perhaps because he became blind as a boy and not after first constituting himself as an adult. Marehu, the best organized of the three, and Muctaru both went blind as adults. Unlike the two of them, Sayo took up the kututeng in a professional manner early in life, since he became blind early. Perhaps Muctaru's more recent blindness, relative to the other two, was something he was still adjusting to when I met him. It is possible that his musical style was still developing while those of the other two musicians were more set.

These lives unfolded during a period of change at Bafodea. In the precontact era, Muctaru would not have gone to Kenema to the school for the blind. The move from the old to the new site of Bafodea Town influenced the kinds of contacts people made with the outside world; the first road was built to Bafodea Town at about the same time the site was moved. I have the sense from talking to Marehu that the move changed the musical scene in Bafodea Town even if it did not alter Marehu's music so much. Yet even he picked up the Maloko form of Kututeng from the radio. Perhaps Sayo would have been the same person if he had lived in precontact times—it is difficult to say. Kututeng is linked closely to change. We have seen how delighted both Sayo and Marehu were, on different occasions, to hear themselves playing on a tape recorder. One wonders whether the recording experience might not eventually have influenced their musicianship.

Thus, the musicians' personal life experiences, coupled with factors of change, influenced both instrumental and vocal Kututeng music in various ways, affecting performance styles and altering and diversifying the culture's music.

Kututeng and the Larger Aesthetic World

Having stressed the similarities and differences in the music and the lives of these three musicians and how they influenced Bafodea musical culture, I now want to return to some general features. Despite their isolation as blind people, including their partial isolation from the normal successes of everyday farming, trade, and politics, these musicians were connected with the larger cultural world in several ways. Being Kututeng players and sometime ensemble performers put them in an accepted, though not high-status, class of musicians in general. And Kututeng was, at times, directly associated with other musical forms and groups through kututeng performers' playing their instruments in Kunkuma and Poro ensembles and through their playing a variety of non-Kututeng music, such as Kunkuma, Poro, Kukangtan, Balanji, and flute forms, solo on the kututeng. (It was relatively easy for kututeng players to imitate both the melodic and rhythmical elements of other forms of music.) Kututeng solo music on occasion was played at the same rites as other music, even if the musician or musicians had not been specifically invited to play. For these reasons, Kututeng music and its instrument were linked with the larger musical scene at Bafodea, even if on something of a peripheral level. Blindness may have isolated some of its players socially, but their isolation did not disconnect Kututeng music itself from the larger world of Bafodea music.

Kututeng at Bafodea was also associated with the larger aesthetic world, beyond that of music alone (Ottenberg n.d.)—the world of visual art designs, which occur as incising on storage boxes, combs, and several types of wood idiophones such as the nkali, in the colorful arrangements on beaded bands (Ottenberg 1992), in female body markings, in designs on aluminum jewelry, in stamped designs on men's clothes, in designs on leather charms, in basketry, and elsewhere. Similarities between Kututeng and visual art include (1) a great deal of repetition of simple underlying elements whose aesthetic interest does not depend upon their building up into complex hierarchies but rather upon the viewer's delight in small variations, (2) an overall simplicity of organization, (3) an ease in learning the necessary skills without a master-apprentice or master-student relationship, (4) a segmental quality, (5) a tendency toward duality or bilateral symmetry, represented in music by the behaviors of musician and responders in the call-and-response relationship, and (6) a lack of rigidity in the rules of procedure—there is tolerance for a great deal of variation in both design and musical motifs. Kututeng music shares these features with most other musical forms at Bafodea and with many visual designs, which places it within the larger fabric of Bafodea aesthetics. True, the blind musicians no longer saw these visual art forms, but they certainly did so when they were young and had sight. Whether they recalled them in blindness or not, the associations between visual and musical forms seem striking to me.

I can extend this argument further to social groupings (Ottenberg n.d.), as others have done for other cultures (Brett-Smith 1984; Fernandez 1971; Kaeppler 1978; Thompson 1974). I suggest that many of these aesthetic patterns are similar to patterns in Bafodea social relationships and organizations, such as the similarity between the relative lack of hierarchy in social life (even though Bafodea is a chiefdom and has village heads) and the relative lack of hierarchy in musical composition. There is also a segmental quality to social groups, particularly to village communities as relatively small, independent units, like the tendency for Bafodea music to be made up of small, rather independent units. There is the duality of political organization in Bafodea as a whole and in many villages, with one dominant patrilineal clan (which varies from community to community) and one or two other clans playing specific balancing roles. This pattern mirrors cooperative call-and-response singing patterns. Moreover, one can see a repetitiveness in social life and in music, yet a lack of rigidity in both realms, allowing for considerable personal variation without many strong taboos that are strictly enforced.

Thus I perceive a larger cultural aesthetic to Bafodea existence that is very general and quite encompassing. Kututeng music is in no way contradictory to it but fits nicely into it. The music is not eccentric to the general cultural and social aesthetic; rather, by its very presence it reinforces this aesthetic's major elements, even though Kututeng musicians are of low status in Bafodea society. This general aesthetic may provide the three players with a sense of identity within the larger culture to counter their feelings of personal isolation from many of its activities. This is so despite differences in their performance styles, techniques, voices, and song texts.

Four Key Features

Although there were, as we have seen, occasional disagreements and unhappy moments between chorus and kututeng player, Kututeng performances on the whole were conflict-free situations in which troubles were put aside and expressed only in song texts. They were moments when everyday time diminished and musical time became prominent. As Blacking (1973:52) writes of Tshikona performances among the Venda: "Old age, death, grief, thirst, hunger, and other afflictions in this world are seen as transitory events. There is freedom from the restrictions of actual time."

This relative freedom from everyday time (Stone 1982:9), with its accompanying sense of community, was one of four key features characterizing Kututeng music at Bafodea. Kututeng performances very much emphasized time through rhythm—through the fingering of the instrument's tongues, the shaking and knocking of the kututeng box, the clapping, and the singing and dancing. These rhythmic elements created a sense of time that overshadowed everyday time in the community.

A second feature is that many of the songs were about conflicts and troubles: problems between lovers, between a husband and his wife's lover, between a married woman and her lover, or among a man's wives. They spoke of jealousies between friends, of concern over witches (whom Bafodeans believe are really other people or their spiritual representatives), and of blindness, death, grief, and illness. Yet the instrumentalists and chorus were happy in a sort of pleasant, timeless musical world. By placing everyday conflict and troubles in the Kututeng musical scene, they were reformulated for a brief period of happiness. They were made harmless and turned into humor, whereas in everyday life, in everyday time, they could be grim. Through the music, a kind of liminal state of *communitas* (Turner 1974) was reached—a social solidarity of joy and cheerfulness in spite of singing about unhappy events.

I think the repetition of songs and of the kututeng's instrumental phrases, along with the common employment of relatively simple song texts that enabled everyone present to participate, played a major role in people's attaining this condition. The repetitions altered normal, everyday time and thought through the process of redundancy (Bateson 1973:240). The simplicity of song content allowed a sense of community to flourish because everyone could understand the nature of the musical activity itself, even if they were not always clear about the meaning of some of the song texts. As Chernoff has written (1979:61): "In traditional African music-making situations, the music is basically familiar, and people can follow with their informed interest the efforts of musicians to add an additional dimension of excitement or depth to a performance. Relatively minor variations stand out clearly and assure increased competence in making the occasion successful." Later he states that an African drummer "uses repetition to reveal the *depths* of the musical structure" (1979:112, italics his)—that is, the emphasis on form is crucial.

A third feature is that the repetitiveness of the instrumental music and song, the steady rhythm, sometimes the repetitive movement of dancers in a circle, and the minimizing of everyday time allowed not only for a sense of momentary social solidarity but also for a special sort of inner individualism. It permitted those at the performance to daydream, which I believe to be one of the major functions of many Bafodea musical events, as it is at Afikpo Igbo masquerades in southeastern Nigeria (Ottenberg 1972:35) and undoubtedly elsewhere. The participants' daydreams might connect with the song text, the dance steps, the social situation, or the people present, or they might range far from any of them. The achievement of a state of community through music allowed individuals to dissociate mentally from the musical group even while performing and interacting within it bodily. As changes occurred in the instrumental playing or the musician's song, or when there was some creativity in either, people who were there might move out of their dissociated state for a time, so that there was a swinging back and forth between full consciousness and daydreaming. Daydreaming might have allowed participants to deal with their fantasies relating to past, present, and future experiences regarding lovers, witches, and other matters raised in the song content. Or the music may have created a temporary state of suspension of thought, when people simply sang and danced.

Individualism in performance within the temporary music community was manifested in the fourth key feature of Kututeng music—its flexibility. The instrumentalist often performed when he wished; people gathered and left as they desired. There was no obligation to take part, to respond to the instrumentalist, or to dance. The musician played whatever form of Kututeng he wished, whether traditional or contemporary. Nevertheless, during a performance there was a good sense of musical and social community. This flexibility stood in some contrast to the situation in which musicians were hired for certain rites and other events: they were expected to play at certain times and to perform the kind of music appropriate for the rite, and others were expected to respond in singing and perhaps in dancing to ensure a proper ritual spirit.

Voluntarism and individuality in initiative and in response are also common in some other areas of Bafodea life, as in deciding when to perform certain rituals such as second burials, in trading, and in the extent of enterprise exerted in marrying and farming. Voluntarism and individuality are accepted social concepts in Bafodea, a society that is neither strongly hierarchical nor rule-ridden. Kututeng music, and to some extent Kunkuma, reflect this voluntaristic aspect of Bafodea society (Merriam 1964:chapter 12), as other music does its more obligatory aspects. Male instrumentalists reflect male dominance in key areas of Bafodea society (Ottenberg 1983); the responders' behavior toward the instrumentalist, in which opinions about him are often freely expressed, mirrors the cooperative responses of women and children to that authority.

The use of the kututeng in the home, on farms, at public rituals, and, at times, in the men's secret society preinitiation rites—all in a rather free manner for instrumentalist and responders—reflects the widespread acceptance of the theme of voluntarism and individual initiative within a society that also stresses group identity. Further, voluntarism and individuality are increasing in Bafodea society as it undergoes contemporary changes. Kututeng music mirrors these changes with its European-produced metal box and umbrella-stay tongues, its occasional use of some Krio words and phrases in song, and the penetration of Kunkuma, Poro, and other outside musical forms into its repertoire. It may be that Western musical influences on Bafodea, exerted through radio, audiotapes, and Bafodeans who have been elsewhere in Sierra Leone, reinforce the popularity of Kututeng music there, for much of the outside music is strong in melodic elements.

As I have already indicated, voluntarism is characteristic of features in other Bafodea art forms as well, as in the choices allowed in designs on wooden boxes, combs, and spoons, beaded bands, and other objects (Ottenberg 1992, n.d.). Design choice is up to the individual creator. For most of these objects, what is required, or perhaps only requested, is that they have *some* design—that initiating girls wear some sort of decorated headband at their dances, that upon marriage a girl brings a decorated wood storage box to her new home.

The individualism and voluntarism involved in Kututeng music, its secular quality, and the topical contents of its songs suggest that it is a form of popular culture, one connected to the larger picture of popular culture in Sierra Leone and its cities (Barber 1987). Certainly Kututeng playing is common in the country, no matter under what name, as are various forms of Kunkuma and Poro, as van Oven's numerous publications attest (1970, 1973-74, 1980, 1981, 1982). Played on the radio, whether in Limba, Lokko, or the language of some other Sierra Leone culture, Kututeng is losing its localism and tribal identity, becoming Sierra Leone music. The Bafodea forms are, in some sense, connected to the popular musical culture of this larger national world. Scholars may tend to think of popular culture as largely urban-based, but it also may have rural roots or it may spread to the rural areas from the urban scene (Ottenberg 1993), as well as the reverse. It becomes so firmly embedded in rural areas like Bafodea chiefdom as to appear traditional to local people as well as to the anthropologist.

Research and Writing Issues

Finally, I want to comment on the form of presentation and analysis employed in this work, particularly its advantages and disadvantages in comparison with other forms of presentation. To me, a powerful advantage is that it places the individual squarely in the understanding of culture, here especially the musical culture of Kututeng and, to some extent, of Kunkuma and other Bafodea musical forms. We see three musicians through their life experiences, particularly those relating to their music and their blindness. We view the musicians as human beings working out roles for themselves in a culture that greatly limits their possibilities. We know them as creative, innovative, assertive individuals re-creating Kututeng musical culture or, in Marehu's case, maintaining tradition. I have tried to link their everyday lives to their performances and personal creativity, which are, in turn, associated with their manipulation of the Kututeng cultural form. They are not passive accepters of a tradition—even in Marehu's case not fully so—but are moving that tradition ahead in different directions.

What influence these three will prove to have on the future of Kututeng music at Bafodea is uncertain. Who among their listeners will take over each musician's particular approach, adding a new individual style to move the Kututeng tradition onward? None of the three musicians had apprentices, but among their listeners or the chorus, individuals may be attracted to the instrument, emulate one of the three, and then develop in their own way. What might be will require further research. As of now, Kututeng at Bafodea is not the same as it was fifty years ago.

Further, in this analysis I have tried as much as possible to make these three musicians' voices heard by reporting on interviews with them, at times quoting what they said, and reproducing the song texts they presented in their performances. I have sometimes placed these items in the context of my interactions with the musicians and of my reactions to them and theirs to me. This internal view—the view of those being researched—has become increasingly vital in anthropology in recent years. The voices of indigenous people must be heard (Geertz 1983). One cannot do proper anthropology without them, and look at the immense riches in understanding they provide!

At the same time, my voice is strongly present in this analysis. I organized the study, and I created an overall structure and field of Kututeng in a way that Bafodeans do not present it to anyone. They, instead, live it and do not have to think about it in my ways. I have to understand it in my own way and translate it into the current terms of an anthropology that originated in the West, where its center still lies. If I asked each of the three musicians to classify his music, I have also made my own classification, sometimes in agreement with theirs, sometimes not, and sometimes extending theirs. If I have noted their interpretations of the song texts, I have sometimes produced my own comments as well. I have engaged in an external-internal dialogue with them through my field notes, films, and tapes (Sanjek 1990), which continues through the writing process.

It is virtually impossible to present an entirely internal, indigenous view in an anthropological analysis. Until recent years the weight has been on the other side: analysis has been too strongly an external conception. The indigenous voice has not been heard well, if at all. I have attempted to achieve a balance between the internal and external views, which has helped me show three individuals in a culture who re-created it, reshaped it, or attempted to maintain it, doing so in a still largely traditionally oriented society. In this they have been assisted and supported by their responders and listeners at performances. What anthropologists must find is a balance between the internal view and their own conception of the culture they are attempting to understand.

A disadvantage of my approach to writing is that it is at least partly a sort of "build up" one. You do not get all the information about the kututeng instrument in one place, but rather as you go along through the discussion of the three musicians. You do not get a general overview of Kututeng music at the beginning as a guide, or a set of categories to be fleshed out in the anthropologist's text. Instead, information about the instrument, music types, songs, and the relationships of the musician to the chorus and listeners emerges gradually through the discussion of each musician in turn. The full picture evolves from the text much as it actually evolved for the anthropologist in the field. Only in this concluding chapter does the larger frame appear fully, as does the probable history of the Kututeng musical form. This approach may be frustrating for those who want immediately to know what the basic forms and performative modes of the music are.

I respect the more traditional form of analysis, as exemplified in the ethnomusicologist Berliner's (1978) study of the Shona mbira, which is excellent in its organization, logical to follow in its musical analysis, and much more technically oriented toward the music than my study is. But I prefer a view of culture that grows more out of the individual, although I am not sure it is the best view for every cultural study, for every purpose. I like the idea that different anthropological approaches may be best suited to different kinds of cultural materials, although I believe the view I have been exploring in this book is within the range of those most fashionable today in anthropology—a discipline of ever-changing scholarly fashions. As I mentioned in an earlier chapter, my approach initially grew out of personal loneliness and sorrow in the field, which connected me with three men who, I believed, had similar feelings to varying degrees. And my lack of technical musical knowledge led me to focus on the lives of these three musicians. So rather than arising from any intellectual conviction that working with and through them was the correct way to do anthropology, my approach arose from my personal experience.

Whatever else this document is, it is about the lives of three men explicitly and about my life by implication. In taking this view I have tried to blend the heart with some contemporary intellectual currents. Both are important: the heart is more often neglected than the scholarly currents. Bateson (1973:235), in discussing the nature of art, argues that "for the attainment of grace, the reasons of the heart must be integrated with the reasons of the reason." That is what I have attempted to do here, with reference to the musicians and their performances and to myself as anthropologist—and all of us as human beings.

References Cited

Akpabot, Samuel. 1971. "African Instrumental Music." *African Arts* 7(1):63–64, 84.

Ames, David W. 1968. "Professional and Amateurs: The Musicians of Zaria and Obimo." *African Arts* 1(2):40–45, 80–84.

———. 1973a. "Igbo and Hausa Musicians: A Comparative Examination." *Ethnomusicology* 17(2):250–78.

———. 1973b. "A Sociological View of Hausa Musical Activity." In Warren L. d'Azevedo (ed.), *The Traditional Artist in African Societies*, 128–61. Bloomington: Indiana University Press.

Anderson, Lois. 1980. "Uganda. I:4 Instruments." In Stanley Sadie (ed.), *The New Grove Dictionary of Music and Musicians*, vol. 19, 313–16. London: Macmillan.

Ankermann, Bernhard. 1901. "Die afrikanischen Musikinstruments." *Ethnologisches Notizblatt* 3(1):1–134. Reprinted 1976. Leipzig: Zentralantiquariat der Deutschen Demokratischen Republik.

Barber, Karin. 1987. "Popular Arts in Africa." *African Studies Review* 30(3):1–78.

Bateson, Gregory. 1973. "Style, Grace, and Information in Primitive Art." In Anthony Forge (ed.), *Primitive Art and Society*, 235–55. London: Oxford University Press.

Bebey, Francis. 1975. *African Music: A People's Art*. Translated by Josephine Bennett. New York: Lawrence Hill.

Becker, Howard S. 1966. *Outsiders: Studies in the Sociology of Deviance*. New York: Free Press.

Berliner, Paul F. 1978. *The Soul of Mbira: Music and Traditions of the Shona People of Zimbabwe*. Berkeley: University of California Press.

Blacking, John. 1961. "Patterns of Nsenga Kalimba Music." *African Music* 2(4):26–43.

———. 1967. *Venda Children's Songs: A Study in Ethnomusicological Analysis*. Johannesburg: Witwatersrand University Press.

———. 1971a. "The Value of Music in Human Experience." In Lexander L. Ringer (ed.), *1969 Yearbook of the International Folk Music Council*, 33–71. Urbana: University of Illinois Press.

———. 1971b. "Music and Historical Process in Vendaland." In Klaus P. Wachsmann (ed.), *Essays on Music and History in Africa*, 185–212. Evanston, Illinois: Northwestern University Press,

———. 1973. *How Musical Is Man?* Seattle: University of Washington Press.

———. 1977. "Towards an Anthropology of the Body." In John Blacking (ed.), *The Anthropology of the Body*, 1–28. Association of Social Anthropologists, Monograph 15. London: Academic Press.

———. 1987. *A Commonsense View of All Music: Reflections on Percy Grainger's Contribution to Ethnomusicology and Music Education.* Cambridge: Cambridge University Press.

Borel, Francois. 1986. *Collection d'instruments du musique les sanza.* Neuchatel: Musée d'Ethnographie, Collections du Musée d'Ethnographie Neuchatel, 2.

Bourdieu, Pierre. 1977. *Outline of a Theory of Practice.* Cambridge: Cambridge University Press.

Brett-Smith, Sarah C. 1984. "Speech Made Visible: The Irregular as a System of Meaning." *Empirical Studies of the Arts* 2(2):127–47.

Brisley, Thomas. 1909. "Some Notes on the Baule Tribe." *Journal of the African Society* 8:296–302.

Büttikofer, Johann. 1890. *Reisebilder aus Liberia: Resultate geographischer, naturwissenschaftlichen und ethnographer Undersuchungen wahrend der Jahre 1879–1882 und 1886–1887.* 2 vols. Leiden: Brill.

Cannizzo, Jeanne. 1978. "Alikali Devils: Children's Masquerades in a West African Town." Ph.D. dissertation, Department of Anthropology, University of Washington.

———. 1979. "The Alikali Devils of Sierra Leone." *African Arts* 12(4):64–70, 90.

Casagrande, Joseph B. (ed.). 1960. *In the Company of Men.* New York: Harper & Row.

Chernoff, John Miller. 1979. *African Rhythm and African Sensibility.* Chicago: University of Chicago Press.

Clarke, Mary Lane. 1922. *A Limba-English Dictionary, or Tampan ta ka talun ta ka Hulimba ha in Huinkilisi ha.* New York: Houghton.

Clifford, James, and George E. Marcus (eds.). 1986. *Writing Culture: The Poetics and Politics of Ethnography.* Berkeley: University of California Press.

Codere, Helen. 1973. *The Biography of an African Society: Rwanda 1900-1960.* Annales, Série en 8, Sciences Humaines 79. Tervuren: Musée Royal de l'Afrique Centrale.

Cooke, Peter. 1980. "Lamellaphone, part 6: Latin America." In Stanley Sadie (ed.), *The New Grove Dictionary of Music and Musicians,* vol. 10, 406-407. London: Macmillan.

Courlander, Harold. 1941. "Musical Instruments of Haiti." *Musical Quarterly* 27(3):371-83.

———. 1942. "Musical Instruments of Cuba." *Musical Quarterly* 28(2):227-40.

Davenport, Peter S. 1984. "Form and Structure in Kondi Music of Northeastern Sierra Leone: Kututeng Music among the Limba." Master's thesis, School of Music, University of Washington.

Drewal, Margaret Thompson. 1991. "The State of Research on Performance in Africa." *African Studies Review* 34(3):1-64.

Echezona, W. W. C. 1980. "Igbo Music." In Stanley Sadie (ed.), *The New Grove Dictionary of Music and Musicians,* vol. 9, 20-23. London: Macmillan.

Erlmann, Veit. 1991. *African Stars: Studies in Black South African Performance.* Chicago: University of Chicago Press.

Fabian, Johannes. 1983. *Time and the Other: How Anthropology Makes Its Object.* New York: Columbia University Press.

Fernandez, James W. 1971. "Principles of Opposition and Vitality in Fang Aesthetics." In Carol F. Jopling (ed.), *Art and Aesthetics in Primitive Societies,* 356-73. New York: Dutton.

Finnegan, R. H. 1965. *Survey of the Limba Peoples of Sierra Leone.* Great Britain, Department of Technical Co-operation, Overseas Research Publications, no. 8. London: Her Majesty's Stationery Office.

———. 1967. *Limba Stories and Story-Telling.* Oxford: Clarendon Press, Oxford Library of African Literature.

———. 1989. *The Hidden Musicians: Music-Making in an English Town.* Cambridge: Cambridge University Press.

Fortes, Meyer. 1973. "On the Concept of the Person among the Talensi." In G. Dieterlen (ed.), *La notion de personne en Afrique noire,* 283-319. Paris: Editions de Centre National de la Recherche Scientifique.

Fox, Lorene K. (ed.). 1967. *East African Childhood: Three Versions.* Nairobi: Oxford University Press.

Frisbie, Charlotte J., and David P. McAllester (eds.). 1978. *Navajo Blessingway Singer: The Autobiography of Frank Mitchell, 1881-1967.* Tucson: University of Arizona Press.

Fyle, Clifford N., and Eldred D. Jones. 1980. *A Krio-English Dictionary.* New York: Oxford University Press.

Gatheru, R. Muto. 1964. *Child of Two Worlds: A Kikuyu's Story.* New York: Praeger.

Geertz, Clifford. 1983. " 'From the Native's Point of View': On the Nature of Anthropological Understanding." In his *Local Knowledge: Further Essays in Interpretative Anthropology,* 55–70. New York: Basic Books.

Giddens, Anthony. 1976. *New Rules of the Sociological Method: A Positive Critique of Interpretative Sociologies.* London: Hutchinson.

———. 1979. *Central Problems in Social Theory: Action, Structure and Contradiction in Social Analysis.* Berkeley: University of California Press.

———. 1981. *A Contemporary Critique of Historical Materialism, vol. 1: Power, Property and the State.* Berkeley: University of California Press.

Goldie, Hugh. 1862. *Dictionary of the Efik Language.* Glasgow: Dunn and Wright.

Hart, W. A. 1989. "Woodcarving of the Limba of Sierra Leone." *African Arts* 23(1):44–53, 103.

Herskovits, Melville J. 1944. "Drums and Drummers in Afro-Brazilian Cult Life." *Musical Quarterly* 30(4):477–92.

Jackson, Michael. 1983. "Knowledge of the Body." *Man* 18(2):327–45.

Jackson, Michael, and Ivan Karp. 1990. "Introduction." In Michael Jackson and Ivan Karp (eds.), *Personhood and Agency: The Experience of Self and Other in African Cultures.* 15–30. Uppsala Studies in Cultural Anthropology 14. Washington, D.C.: Smithsonian Institution Press, and Stockholm: Almqvist & Wiksell.

John, J. T. 1952. "Village Music in Sierra Leone." *West African Review* 23:1043, 1045, 1071.

Jones, A. M. 1950. "The Kalimba of the Lala Tribe of Northern Rhodesia." *Africa* 20(4):324–34.

———. 1954. "African Rhythm." *Africa* 24(1):26–47.

———. 1964. *Africa and Indonesia: The Evidence of the Xylophone and Other Cultural Factors.* Leiden: Brill.

Jones, Eldred. 1968. "Freetown: The Contemporary Scene." In Christopher Fyle and Eldred Jones (eds.), *Freetown: A Symposium,* 199–211. Freetown: Sierra Leone Universities Press.

Kaeppler, Adrienne. 1978. "Melody, Drone and Decoration: Underlying Structures and Surface Manifestations in Tongan Art and Society." In Michael Greenhalgh and Vincent Megaw (eds.), *Art in Society,* 261–74. New York: St. Martin's.

Karp, Ivan. 1986. "Agency and Social Theory: A Review of Anthony Giddens." *American Ethnologist* 13(1):131–37.

Kauffman, Robert A. 1980. Introductory section to "Lamellaphone." In Stanley Sadie (ed.), *The New Grove Dictionary of Music and Musicians,* vol. 10, 401–402. London: Macmillan.

Kauffman, Robert A., Gerhard Kubik, Anthony King, and Peter Cooke. 1980. "Lamellaphone." In Stanley Sadie (ed.), *The New Grove Dictionary of Music and Musicians.* London: Macmillan. vol. 10, 401–407.

Keil, Charles. 1979. *Tiv Song.* Chicago: University of Chicago Press.

Kelley, Jane Holden. 1978. *Yaqui Women: Contemporary Life Histories.* Lincoln: University of Nebraska Press.

Kennedy, John G. T. 1977. *Struggle for Change in a Nubian Community: An Individual in Society and History.* Palo Alto, California: Mayfield Publishing Company.

King, Anthony. 1980. "Lamellaphone, part 5: West Africa." In Stanley Sadie (ed.), *The New Grove Dictionary of Music and Musicians,* vol. 10, 406. London: Macmillan.

Kreutzinger, Helga. 1966. *The Eri Devils in Freetown, Sierra Leone.* Ethnologica et Linguistica, no. 9. Vienna: Osterrichische Ethnologische Gesellschaft.

Kubik, Gerhard. 1964. "Generic Names for the Mbira." *African Music* 3(3):25–36.

————. 1977. "Patterns of Body Movement in the Music of Boys' Initiation in South-East Angola." In John Blacking (ed.), *The Anthropology of the Body,* 253–74. Association of Social Anthropologists, Monograph 15. London: Academic Press.

————. 1980a. "Lamellaphone, part 2: Marimba Types; part 3: Mbira Types; part 4: Likembe Types." In Stanley Sadie (ed.), *The New Grove Dictionary of Music and Musicians,* vol. 10, 402–406. London: Macmillan.

————. 1980b. "Tanzania." In Stanley Sadie (ed.), *The New Grove Dictionary of Music and Musicians,* vol. 18, 567–71. London: Macmillan.

Lamm, Judith Ann. 1968. "Musical Instruments of Sierra Leone." Master's thesis, Department of Music, University of Wisconsin.

Langness, L. L. 1965. *The Life History in Anthropological Science.* New York: Holt, Rinehart and Winston.

Langness, L. L., and Gelya Frank. 1981. *Lives: An Anthropological Approach to Life History.* Novato, California: Chandler and Sharp.

Laurenty, J. S. 1962. *Les sanzas du Congo.* 2 vols. Annales, Série en 4, Sciences Humaines 3. Tervuren: Musée Royal de l'Afrique Centrale.

Leis, Philip E. 1972. *Enculturation and Socialization in an Ijaw Village.* New York: Holt, Rinehart and Winston.

Lewis, Oscar. 1961. *Children of Sanchez: Autobiography of a Mexican Family.* New York: Random House.

Luthali, Albert. 1962. *Let My People Go: An Autobiography.* Johannesburg: Collins.

MacLeod, Bruce A. 1993. *Club Date Musicians: Playing the New York Party Circuit.* Urbana: University of Illinois Press.

Maraire, Abraham Dumisani. 1990. "The Position of Music in Shona *Mudzimu* (Ancestral Spirit) Possession." Ph.D. dissertation, Department of Music, University of Washington.

Mead, Margaret. 1928. *Coming of Age in Samoa.* New York: Morrow.

———. 1930. *Growing Up in New Guinea.* New York: Morrow.

Merriam, Alan P. 1962. "The African Idiom in Music." *Journal of American Folklore* 75(296):120–30.

———. 1964. *The Anthropology of Music.* Evanston, Illinois: Northwestern University Press.

———. 1973. "The Bala Musician." In Warren L. d'Azevedo (ed.), *The Traditional Artist in African Societies,* 250–81. Bloomington: Indiana University Press.

———. 1977. "Music Change in Basonge Village." *Anthropos* 72:806–46.

———. 1979. "Basongye Musicians and Institutionalized Social Deviance." *Yearbook of the International Folk Music Council* 11:1–26.

Merrill, William L. 1988. *Rarámuri Souls: Knowledge and Social Process in Northern Mexico.* Washington, D.C.: Smithsonian Institution Press.

Migeod, Frederick Hugh William. 1927. *A View of Sierra Leone.* New York: Brentano's.

Mintz, Sidney. 1960. *Worker in the Cane Field.* New Haven, Connecticut: Yale University Press.

Montandon, George. 1919. "La généalogie des instruments du musique et les cycles de civilisation." *Archives Suisses d'Anthropologie Générale* 3(1):1–120.

Moore, Carlos. 1982. *Fela, Fela, This Bitch of a Life.* London: Allison and Busby.

Nettl, Bruno. 1983. *The Study of Ethnomusicology.* Urbana: University of Illinois Press.

Nketia, J. H. Kwabena. 1963. *African Music in Ghana.* Evanston, Illinois: Northwestern University Press.

———. 1973. "The Musician in Akan Society." In Warren L. d'Azevedo (ed.), *The Traditional Artist in African Societies*, 79–100. Bloomington: Indiana University Press.

———. 1974. *The Music of Africa*. New York: Norton.

———. 1980. "Ghana." In Stanley Sadie (ed.), *The New Grove Dictionary of Music and Musicians*, vol. 7, 326–32. London: Macmillan.

Nunley, John W. 1987. *Moving with the Face of the Devil: Art and Politics in Urban West Africa*. Urbana: University of Illinois Press.

Okafor-Omali, Dilim. 1965. *A Nigerian Villager in Two Worlds*. London: Faber and Faber.

Okosa, A. N. G. 1962. "Ibo Musical Instruments." *Nigeria Magazine* 75:4–14.

Omibiyi, Mosunmola. 1977. "Nigerian Musical Instruments." *Nigeria Magazine* 122/123:14–34.

Oppong, Christine. 1973. *Growing Up in Dagbon*. Accra: Ghana Publishing Corporation.

Ottenberg, Simon. 1968. *Double Descent in an African Society: The Afikpo Village-Group*. American Ethnological Society, Monograph Series, no. 47. Seattle: University of Washington Press.

———. 1971. *Leadership and Authority in an African Society: The Afikpo Village-Group*. American Ethnological Society, Monograph Series, no. 52. Seattle: University of Washington Press.

———. 1972. "Humorous Masks and Serious Politics at Afikpo." In Douglas Fraser and Herbert M. Cole (eds.), *African Art and Leadership*, 91–121. Madison: University of Wisconsin Press.

———. 1975. *The Masked Rituals of Afikpo: The Context of an African Art*. Seattle: University of Washington Press.

———. 1982. "Illusion, Communication, and Psychology in West African Masquerades." *Ethos* 10(2):149–85.

———. 1983. "Artistic and Sex Roles in a Limba Chiefdom." In Christine Oppong (ed.), *Female and Male in West Africa*, 76–90. London: Allen and Unwin.

———. 1986. "Two New Religions, One Analytic Frame." *Cahiers d'Études Africaines* 96:437–54.

———. 1988a. "The Bride Comes to the Groom: Ritual and Drama in Limba Weddings." *The Drama Review* 32(2):42–62.

———. 1988b. "Religion and Ethnicity in the Arts of a Limba Chiefdom." *Africa* 58(4):437–65.

———. 1989a. *Boyhood Rituals in an African Society: An Interpretation*. Seattle: University of Washington Press.

————. 1989b. "The Dancing Bride: Art and Indigenous Psychology in Limba Weddings." *Man* 24:57–78.

————. 1989c. "We Are Becoming Art Minded: Afikpo Arts 1988." *African Arts* 22(4):58–67.

————. 1989d. "Return to the Field: Anthropological Déjà-vu." *Cambridge Anthropology* 12:16–31.

————. 1990. "Thirty Years of Fieldnotes: Changing Relationships to the Text." In Roger Sanjek (ed.), *Fieldnotes: The Makings of Anthropology,* 139–60. Ithaca, New York: Cornell University Press.

————. 1992. "The Beaded Bands of Bafodea." *African Arts* 25(2):64–75, 98–99.

————. 1993. "One Face of a Culture: Two Musical Ensembles in a Limba Chiefdom, Sierra Leone." In Regis Antoine (ed.), *Carrefour de cultures: Mélanges offerts à Jacqueline Leiner,* 57–75. Études Littéraires Françaises, no. 55. Tubingen: Éditions Gunter Narr.

————. 1994a. "Male and Female Secret Societies among the Bafodea Limba of Northern Sierra Leone." In Thomas D. Blakely, Walter E. C. van Beek, and Dennis L. Thomson (eds.), *Religion in Africa: Experience and Expression,* 363–87. Monograph Series of the David M. Kennedy Center for International Studies at Brigham Young University, no. 4. London: James Curry, and Portsmouth, New Hampshire: Heinemann.

————. 1994b. "Changes over Time in an African Culture and in an Anthropologist." In Don D. Fowler and Donald L. Hardesty (eds.), *Others Knowing Others: Perspectives on Ethnographic Careers,* 91–118. Washington, D.C.: Smithsonian Institution Press.

————. n.d. "Design and Song in a Limba Chiefdom." Unpublished manuscript.

Radin, Paul. 1926. *Crashing Thunder: The Autobiography of an American Indian.* New York: Appleton.

Raum, Otto. 1940. *Chaga Childhood.* London: Oxford University Press.

Read, Margaret. 1959. *Children of Their Fathers: Growing Up Among the Ngoni of Nyasaland.* London: Methuen.

Riesman, Paul. 1977. *Freedom in Fulani Social Life: An Introspective Ethnography.* Translated by M. Fuller. Chicago: University of Chicago Press.

————. 1986. "The Person and the Life Cycle in African Social Life and Thought." *African Studies Review* 29(2):71–198.

Rosellini, Jim. 1980. "Upper Volta." In Stanley Sadie (ed.), *The New Grove Dictionary of Music and Musicians,* vol. 19, 456–60. London: Macmillan.

Sahlins, Marshall. 1976. *Culture and Practical Reason.* Chicago: University of Chicago Press.

Sallée, Pierre. 1980. "Gabon." In Stanley Sadie (ed.), *The New Grove Dictionary of Music and Musicians,* vol. 7, 49-54. London: Macmillan.

Sanjek, Roger (ed). 1990. *Fieldnotes: The Makings of Anthropology.* Ithaca: Cornell University Press.

Schaeffner, André. 1951. *Les Kissi: Une société noire et ses instruments de musique.* L'Homme, Cahiers d'Ethnologie, de Géographie et de Linguistique, 2. Paris: Hermann, Actualités Scientifiques et Industrielles, 1139.

Schutz, Alfred. 1951. "Making Music Together: A Study in Social Relationships." *Social Research* 18:76-97.

Selormey, Francis. 1966. *The Narrow Path: An African Childhood.* New York: Praeger.

Senoga-Zake, G. 1986. *Folk Music of Kenya.* Nairobi: Uzima Press.

Shrimpton, Neville. 1987. "Thomas Decker and the Death of Boss Coker." *Africa* 57(4):531-45.

Sievers, Bernard. 1992. *Musik in Sierra Leone: Tradition, Wandel und Identitäts—verlust einer Musikkultur in West-Afrika.* Münster: Lit Verlag, Musik-ethnologie Band 1.

Simmons, Leo W. 1942. *Sun Chief: The Autobiography of a Hopi Man.* New Haven, Connecticut: Yale University Press.

Smith, Mary. 1954. *Baba of Karo.* London: Faber.

Soderberg, Bertil. 1972. "Ornamentation of the Sansa." *African Arts* 5(4):29-33, 88.

Speed, Clarke. 1991. "Swears and Swearing among the Landogo of Northern Sierra Leone: Adjudicating, Aesthetics, and Philosophy of Power." Ph.D. dissertation, Department of Anthropology, University of Washington.

Ssempeke, Albert (as told to Klaus P. Wachsmann). 1975. "The Autobiography of an African Musician." *Music Education Journal* 61(6):52-59.

Staub, J. 1936. *Beitrage zur kenntnis der materiellen Kultur der Mendi.* Separate-Abdruck aus dem Jahrbuch des Bernischen Historischen Museums in Bern, Ethnographische Abteilung XV, Jahrgang 1935. Bern: K. J. Wyss Erben Aktiengesellschaft.

Stone, Ruth. 1980. "Liberia." In Stanley Sadie (ed.), *The New Grove Dictionary of Music and Musicians,* vol. 10, 715-19. London: Macmillan.

———. 1982. *Let the Inside Be Sweet: The Interpretation of Music Event among the Kpelle of Liberia.* Bloomington: Indiana University Press.

Surugue, B. 1980. "Songhay." In Stanley Sadie (ed.), *The New Grove Dictionary of Music and Musicians*, vol. 18, 523-24. London: Macmillan.

Thieme, Darius L. 1967. "Three Yoruba Members of the Mbira-Sanza Family." *Journal of the International Folk Music Council* 19:42-48.

Thompson, David. 1975-76. "A New World Mbira: The Caribbean Marimbula." *African Music* 5(4):140-48.

Thompson, Robert Farris. 1974. *African Art in Motion: Icon and Act.* Los Angeles: University of California Press.

Tracey, Andrew. 1961. "The Mbira Music of Jege A. Tapera." *African Music* 2(4):44-63.

————. 1970. *How to Play the Mbira.* Roodepoort, Transvaal: International Library of African Music.

————. 1972. "The Original African Mbira." *African Music* 5(2):85-104.

Tracey, Hugh. 1961. "A Case for the Name Mbira." *African Music* 2(4):17-25.

Trowell, Margaret, and K. F. Wachsmann. 1953. *Tribal Crafts of Uganda.* London: Oxford University Press.

Turay, A. K. 1966. "A Vocabulary of Temne Musical Instruments." *Sierra Leone Language Review* 5:27-33.

Turner, Victor. 1974. *Drama, Fields, and Metaphors: Symbolic Action in Human Society.* Ithaca, New York: Cornell University Press.

Uku, Edward Kanu. 1993. *Seeds in the Palm of Your Hand,* edited by Mary Easterfield. Madison: University of Wisconsin, African Studies Program.

Underhill, Ruth. 1936. *The Autobiography of a Papago Woman.* Menasha, Wisconsin: American Anthropological Association, Memoir 46.

Vander, Judith. 1988. *Songprints: The Musical Experience of Five Shoshone Women.* Urbana: University of Illinois Press.

van Oven, Cootje. 1962. "Letter to the Editor." *African Music* 3:1, 112.

————. 1970. "Music of Sierra Leone." *African Arts* 3(4):20-27, 71.

————. 1973-74. "The Kondi of Sierra Leone." *African Music* 5(3):77-85.

————. 1980. "Sierra Leone." In Stanley Sadie (ed.), *The New Grove Dictionary of Music and Musicians,* vol. 17, 302-304. London: Macmillan.

————. 1981. *An Introduction to the Music of Sierra Leone.* Self-published.

————. 1982. *Supplement to an Introduction to the Music of Sierra Leone.* Self-published.

von Hornbostel, E. M. 1933. "The Ethnology of African Sound Instruments." *Africa* 8:277-311.

Wachsmann, Klaus. 1970. "Ethnomusicology in Africa." In John N. Paden and Edward W. Soja (eds.), *The African Experience,* vol. 1, 128-51. Evanston, Illinois: Northwestern University Press.

———. 1980. "Uganda. II: Buganda." In Stanley Sadie (ed.), *The New Grove Dictionary of Music and Musicians,* vol. 19, 316-19. London: Macmillan.

Waterman, Christopher. 1990. *Juju: A Social History and Ethnography of an African Popular Music.* Chicago: University of Chicago Press.

Waterman, Richard. 1956. "Music in Australian Aboriginal Culture: Some Sociological and Psychological Implications." *Music Therapy* 1955:40-49.

Winter, Edward H. 1959. *Beyond the Mountains of the Moon: Lives of Four Africans.* Urbana: University of Illiois Press.

Winterbottom, Thomas. 1969 [1803]. *An Account of the Native Africans in the Neighborhood of Sierra Leone.* London: Frank Cass.

Zemp, Hugo. 1964. "Musiciens autochtones et griots Malinke chez les Dan de Côte d'Ivoire." *Cahiers d'Études Africaines* 15:370-82.

———. 1967. "Comment en devient musicien: Quatre exemples de l'ouest Africain." In Tolia Nikiprowetzky (ed.), *La musique dans la vie,* vol. 1, 77-103. Paris: Office de Cooperation Radiophonique.

———. 1971. *Musique Dan.* Paris: Mouton, Cahiers de l'Homme, Ethnologie-Géographie-Linguistique, n.s. 11.

———. 1980. "Ivory Coast." In Stanley Sadie (ed.), *The New Grove Dictionary of Music and Musicians,* vol. 9, 430-34. London: Macmillan.

Discography

Berliner, Paul. 1973. *The Soul of Mbira Tradition of the Shona People of Rhodesia*. Recorded in Rhodesia by Paul Berliner. New York: Nonesuch Records, H-72054.

———. 1977. *Africa: Shona Mbira Music Recorded in Mondoro and Highfields by Paul Berliner*. New York: Nonesuch Records, H-72077.

Jenkins, Jean. 1979. *Sierra Leone: Musiques traditionelles*. Paris: Ocora, Ocora 558549.

Maraire, Abraham Dumisani. 1971. *The African Mbira: Music of the Shona People of Rhodesia*. New York: Nonesuch Records, H-72043.

———. n.d. *African Story Songs Told and Sung by Abraham Dumisani Maraire*. Seattle: University of Washington Press.

van Oven, Cootje. 1981. Cassette tape accompanying *An Introduction to the Music of Sierra Leone*. Self-published.

Zemp, Hugo. n.d.a. *Music of the Dan*. Baren Reiter Musicaphon. UNESCO Collection. An Anthology of African Music. BM30 L 2301.

———. n.d.b. *Ivory Coast. Baule Vocal Music*. Emi-Odeon, 3 CO64-17842.

Index

African piano, 3
"Agency," 6–9, 186–89
American Wesleyan Methodist mission, 34, 138, 167–68
Ames, David: musical studies of, 5, 19, 65
Ankermann, Bernhard, 185

Bafodea chiefdom. *See* Wara Wara Bafodea chiefdom
Bafodea Town: location, 29; research in, 39; old town, 137, 138, 167–68; and new *kututeng* music, 137
balanji music, 38, 160–61, 165
Becker, Howard: study of Chicago jazz players, 22
Berliner, Paul, 4, 19
Blacking, John: folk music concepts of, 21, 191; repetition of song words, 120
Blindness: cause of, 51; and children, 64–66, 173–74; in musicians, 170, 172–74. *See also* Kamara, Sayo; Mansaray, Marehu; Mansaray, Muctaru
bondo women's society: music of, 38, 77; initiation, 77, 179

Children: *kututeng* players and,

172–75. *See also* Kamara, Sayo; Mansaray, Marehu; Mansaray, Muctaru
Chorus. *See* Responders

Dancing: *warana*, 76, 117–18, 126; *kukangtan*, 123; *kunkuma*, 124, 147, 150, 154; *tindotin*, 126–27; *kudingpon*, 127; *kuberiberi*, 127–28, 165; *gbondokali*, 128; *poro*, 124, 129; Rainbow, 132; *maloko*, 164; *marahasi*, 165; preinitiation, 174
Davenport, Peter S.: on Bafodea music, 5; on music in outlying villages, 39–40; and *kututeng*, 72, 73, 122; on Marehu Mansaray's abilities, 159, 164
Disassociated state, 120–22, 193
Drums. *See huban* (musical instrument); *kusung* drum

Farm music, 38, 56–63, 96, 138, 168–69
Finnegan, Ruth: oral literature studies of Limba, 21; Milton Keynes study, 21–22
Flute. *See kuthothiya* flute
Fula, 141; Muslims, 31; musical groups, 39